TABLE OF CONTENTS

VOLUME ONE

USA

Dream Big!!
Barbara [illegible]
USA Taekwondo Captain

BOB SCHALLER

THE OLYMPIC DREAM AND SPIRIT VOLUME 1

Bob Schaller, The Olympic Dream and Spirit Volume 1

ISBN 1-929478--06-2

Ex-Husker Press a Division of Cross Training Publishing
P.O. Box 1541
Grand Island, NE 68802
(800) 430-8588

This book is manufactured in the United States of America.

Library of Congress Cataloging in Publication Data in Progress.

Published by Ex-Husker Press a Division of Cross Training Publishing
P.O. Box 1541
Grand Island, NE 68802
1-800-430-8588

Preface By Bob Schaller

If you could sit down with Mary Lou Retton, Dan O'Brien or any other elite-level athlete, what questions would you ask them?

My goal in *The Olympic Dream and Spirit* series of books was to talk with these athletes about things of great importance in their lives. In these three books, hear what the athletes themselves have to say about their Olympic journeys, and the challenges they've had to overcome, what they've learned about themselves and life from these journeys, and how lessons from sports translate to life.

This is the first time these athletes have shared these very personal stories, and the outcome, whether it was positive or negative.

Almost all of these athletes share two common characteristics: First, they surround themselves with positive-thinking people, because one negative person can spoil the goals and focus of the group. Second, they all believe that adversity can be turned into a positive. That kind of attitude, plus an incredible drive to succeed, has made these athletes winners not just in sports, but in life as well.

CLIFF MEIDL
CANOE/KAYAK

Name: Cliff Meidl
Sport: Canoe/Kayak K-4 1000 meters
Born: March 6, 1966, Hollywood, California
Family: Mother, Senta; Father, Helmut; Brother, Norman
Resides: Redondo Beach, California
Occupation: Financial Consultant
Hometown: Manhattan Beach, California
Trains: Newport Beach, California
Coach: Jerzey Dziadkowiec

Accomplishments: 1996 Olympian; won silver in K-1 1,000m at the 1999 Sprint National Championships; member of the 1999 world championships team, Pan American Games team and European Tour team; won a bronze medal at the international regatta in Slovakia in 1999; won a gold medal in K-2 1,000m at the 1999 team trials; qualified for eight finals at the 1998 Eddie Bauer National Championships; qualified for three finals at the international regatta in Poland in 1996; won a medal of each color at the 1995 Olympic Festival in Colorado

Hobbies: Canoeing, kayaking, reading, watching movies

Post-Olympic goals and plans: I would like to continue my education, receive a master's in Business Administration, and raise a family.

By Cliff Meidl

In 1986, I worked for a construction company as an apprentice plumber, and I also did some extra work in Southern California. One day, as I jackhammered through concrete, I hit three electrical cables, each of which carried approximately 4,160 volts. The initial shock threw me out of the ditch were I was working, leaving the jackhammer lodged vertically between the electrical cables.

I was unconscious, and my body slid back into the ditch where my legs came in contact with the electrical cables. Witnesses said I was shocked for more than 30 seconds. Luckily, the large amounts of electricity traveling through the wires caused a trip in a nearby circuit breaker. During the accident, I received more than 30,000 volts of electricity.

The shock knocked me unconscious and threw my heart into cardiac arrest. A coworker attempted to free me from the electrical cables using the hose from an air compressor. Fortunately, there was a fire station nearby, and firemen were on the scene within minutes to perform life-saving CPR. I went into cardiac arrest again en route to the hospital and then a third time upon arrival.

I was fortunate to be at a "prime age" of 20, so my heart was able to survive all the stress. Usually, when a heart stops under such conditions, the person dies. I had to wonder why I survived through 30,000 volts of electricity and three heart attacks. Either a weed cannot be killed, or someone wanted me around.

I do not remember anything about the accident because it happened so quickly. It occurred about 7 a.m. and I did not wake up until 10 p.m. When I regained consciousness the first time, my parents had to explain what had happened.

I can remember my chest felt as if a truck had run over me. Apparently, during the CPR, cartilage was loosened in my chest, and the pain was intense.

My injuries from the shock were severe. Most of the damage was done to my knees where they came in contact with the jackhammer. More than one-third of the bone in my left knee disintegrated, and the right knee had bone and other tissue damage.

I also had suffered deep tissue burns in my back, head, and toes. Apparently, as the electricity traveled through my body it exited at those points. The doctors had not experienced many situations like this, so the prognosis was uncertain. Several hours after the accident, I was transferred to a specialized burn center where I stayed for three weeks. I was in and out of surgery for 15 days as the doctors tried to assess the extent of my injuries.

The doctors considered amputating both of my legs, but my parents refused that option. Mom and Dad were able to contact a plastic surgeon, Malcolm Lessavoy, at UCLA Medical Center. His plan was to remove a portion of both calf muscles and transplant them onto the burned-away areas of my knees. It was a revolutionary kind of surgery—an experimental process.

At that point, it looked like I might never walk again. I thought, "Well, at least I've kept my legs." I was able to use a wheelchair initially, and after a few months I advanced to crutches. It took almost three years for the injuries to heal and a certain amount of the damage is permanent.

I firmly believe that when an individual goes through a traumatic experience, it builds character within him. He has to keep moving forward and set goals along the way. Every goal he sets and accomplishes should be rewarding. I like to use different role models for different goals; it seems to be more realistic and easier to apply to life.

The rehabilitation was a slow and extensive process. The accident left me with limited use of my legs. I was unable to compete in any sports involving running, and walking itself was a challenge. I had been physically active as a child, and that helped my recovery. I was able to apply my competitive instincts from sports to my rehabilitation process. Every little hurdle turned into a competition.

In the early stages of rehabilitation, I developed a lot of persistence in wanting to get back to a normal life as soon as possible. I did not take "no" for an answer. I had to do my best, and then do a little more.

Hobbling around on crutches was not a bad thing. At first, I moved at a snail's pace. I turned it into a sporting event—eventually, I could cross the college campus at Long Beach State faster than anyone else could walk it. Soon I was actually sprinting on my crutches. I made up those challenges for myself.

I never intended to get involved in competitive canoeing. Since

I could not run, I thought canoeing (an upper-body sport) would be perfect for me. It brought me new challenges and I developed support from surrounding teammates. After paddling canoes for several years, I was introduced to Olympic kayaker Greg Barton, who was performing at a canoe race in California. His accomplishments in kayaking and canoeing motivated me and I used him as a role model.

This motivation led me to start kayak racing, which would be added to my rehabilitation process. After three years of kayaking, I developed a real love for the sport. Even today, kayaking always gives me new challenges. Every day seems to be part of a learning process.

When I was younger, I never thought that some day I would be in the Olympics. I had never even heard of flatwater sprint kayaking. This level of competition developed because I was pursuing new challenges. I saw avenues and pursued them, and finally doors opened. I have to take advantage of opportunities and go through the doors. What began as rehabilitation for my injuries developed into a commitment to reach my ultimate goal. When I reached and achieved one goal, I wanted a higher one. All of a sudden, the level I reached was not good enough, and I pushed myself to the next level.

I believe technique can be taught, but intensity cannot be. Technique has been a challenge throughout my life. I always have had to work a little harder, but the intensity came a lot easier for me. This really helped me get through adversities. I have always wanted to do better, and as I worked harder my dreams grew. My dream came true by competing in the 1996 Olympic Games in Atlanta.

It meant a lot for me to be in the Olympics. I was very proud and honored to represent the United States in the 1996 Games. It is difficult to describe that feeling. I remember sitting at the starting line of my first race in the Olympics as the announcer called our lane assignments. Hearing him say, "U.S.A. lane 5," was amazing. It was awesome to be able to experience that level and race in the Olympics.

I remember another situation—walking into the opening ceremonies at the Olympics. That, too, is a hard feeling to describe in words. It is like the ultimate endorphin rush running through your body.

Being an American means a lot for many reasons. One reason is our medical sophistication. I was very fortunate that we have fast emergency response and medical technology. Many people told me that if my accident had happened in another country, I might have been a goner.

The Olympics may not have been a reality for me had I not been involved in the accident. The opportunities and motivation toward achieving specific goals, such as competing in the Olympics, may not have developed. I may have traveled down other roads and pursued goals and dreams that would have complemented my physical and mental conditions. In many ways, the success in one's achievements should be valued by how one can use his resources.

Presently, my injuries as a result of the accident have not changed. I have been able to strengthen the areas of weakness by weight training and cross training. Periodically, I have used crutches after knee surgeries, and, at some point, I may have knee replacement surgery. However, there is no reason for that now as I am walking well enough. Also, I do not want to incur any more risks related to another surgery.

I know some people think I have a challenge because of my legs. I don't look at it that way. Mine is a small hurdle I have to deal with periodically. I feel for the kids who have real handicaps. It is vital to make them feel important and to help them realize their own potential.

When I talk to kids, the most important thing I tell them is to maximize themselves as individuals. Do not think you have to be a Michael Jordan. Take what you are good at and apply yourself in that area. That is what success is. It is not money—it is what you can achieve. You can relate that to sports—some people are cut out for pro sports or the Olympics, and some are not. Genetics help to some extent. The rest is hard work and dedication. You do not have to go to that extent in your sport. Nevertheless, in life, you work hard and do the best you can.

LAURA WILKINSON
DIVING

Name: Laura Wilkinson
Sport: Diving
Born: Nov. 17, 1977, Houston, Texas
Family: Parents, Ed and Linda; Brother, Rob
Hometown: Houston, Texas
Resides: The Woodlands, Texas
Trains: The Woodlands, Texas
Coach: Kenny Armstrong

Accomplishments: Gold medalist, 1999 U.S. nationals (10-meter platform), silver medalist (3-meter springboard); 1999 Big XII Champion, 10-meter, 3-meter; Goodwill Games gold medalist 10-meter platform (only American male or female to win Goodwill Games gold medal in diving); seven-time national champion; 1998 world championships, fifth place

Hobbies: Reading, drawing, spending time with friends

Post-Olympic goals and plans: See how diving goes, ponder options

By Laura Wilkinson

I used to be a gymnast. I tried a variety of sports and activities while growing up, and when I was 15 I tried diving.

It was kind of weird because I was afraid of activities that required movements of jumping and landing, but I loved diving. I liked landing on my head—it seemed more natural than landing on my feet. On top of that, diving came to me more easily and more quickly than gymnastics.

My competitive diving career consisted of the smaller Junior Olympic meets. That's what I did in high school, because our high school coach didn't want divers on the swimming team.

I kept improving throughout my high school years. A lot of the divers ahead of me accepted scholarships to various colleges. After my senior year, I went to several international competitions, which helped get me noticed by college coaches. Soon I narrowed the list to Ohio State, Tennessee, and Texas. I was excited because they were great teams, and great schools. I picked Texas. I knew the Longhorns had a great swimming team, but I didn't know what to expect in terms of diving.

The best part of being at Texas my freshman year was that four divers, half of the team, were freshmen. It was good that we came in together and I think it helped all of us. Our coach, Matt Scoggin, was pretty new, too, so it was a great situation for us to grow together.

College diving involved a completely different work ethic. I had never lifted weights and it was difficult to balance school and diving at first. I learned time management, which is very important. My first college season went very well and I was able to compete at the NCAA Championships.

At the end of my freshman year, one of my best friends and teammates on The Woodlands team died in a car accident on May 4, 1997. Hilary Grivich was an outstanding gymnast who had competed at the 1992 Olympic Trials and was an alternate. She joined the diving team at The Woodlands right after I did. Hilary, who went to the University of Houston, was just a great person.

She died right before the summer nationals. She was such a big part of our team, The Woodlands team. She was the glue that held us all together. She provided the comic relief and she was everyone's best friend. She always called to get us all together to do things. It was hard on all of us to lose her, though it brought our team together. At the nationals, we were all carrying a lot of emotion because we missed Hilary and wished she could be there. We had leaned on one another so much for support that our bond was strong. Before the meet, I pulled everyone to the side.

"I don't care what happens because we've been through so much," I told my teammates. "I'm going to try my best as a way to thank all of you. You all mean so much to me."

I won my first national title. My aunt, Carolyn Lynch, whom I was very close to, was ill but she was able to see the meet on tape, which was very special. My grandmother was also able to see the meet, which also meant a lot.

Aunt Carolyn had a lot of medical problems. She and my grandmother, along with my mother, of course, always came to my meets. My aunt and I were fascinated with angels and we often sent cards to each other with angels on them.

Aunt Carolyn had a kidney transplant, which carried an 80-percent survival rate. She went on a trip with my grandma to New Mexico and we thought everything was fine. But my aunt went to sleep one night and didn't wake up. So, five months to the day after Hilary died, my aunt died. We had thought the kidney problems would take a toll over time, but suddenly she was gone.

The following year, diving was going well but I was still struggling, as I do to this day, with the deaths of Aunt Carolyn and Hilary. That pain worsened when my grandmother passed away. She had lived close to our family while we were growing up, so I had been blessed to spend a lot of time with her. I felt horrible for my mother because she lost her sister and her mother within a year. Her father died when I was 13, so she has already had more than her share of losses.

When my grandmother died in November 1998, I had planned to be home because I had been to several meets. It was the weekend after my birthday. I got home on a Saturday and my grandma had been taken to the hospital the night before. She was in a coma and I wasn't able to speak with her a final time. That's the rough part. I have not been able to say good-bye to any of the people I've lost. In all three cases, I was due to see them in the coming days, but it seemed I was always a few days too late.

My grandmother, Aunt Carolyn, and my mother always supported me. When it seemed like I couldn't do anything right, they said, "We believe in you." That meant the world to me. I was so lucky to have them there. I am also lucky to have two parents who love me very much and have been supportive in the best possible way my entire life.

I don't know that I've really dealt with the losses. I still go to the cemetery and talk to my aunt. There's a statue of an angel there and that makes me feel better. It just takes a long time to heal things like that.

The deaths always came after I had been through some sort of triumph. Every time something good happened, something bad happened. The NCAA Championships were in March 1997 and not long thereafter Hilary was killed. In August 1997 I won my first nationals and a few months later my aunt died.

The deaths of those three wonderful people taught me a lot. I don't take anything for granted. I never put off seeing someone, or even calling someone back. I try to give more of myself now and appreciate what everyone has given to me. When I get angry, I dismiss it. I just can't hold grudges because it's not worth missing out on another memory. It's made me a lot stronger.

I've gone through many phases as a competitor. I have never had a lot of confidence in myself, so it's been a tremendous learning process to believe in my ability. We won't go anywhere if we don't start out with a great belief in ourselves.

Kenny Armstrong and Matt Scoggin, my coaches, have been great. Kenny was there from the start. He said, "Maybe you don't believe in yourself, but I know what you can do." I figured, "If I can't trust my coaches, who can I trust?" So I believed in them, and the confidence came.

My belief and confidence went through the ultimate change at the 1998 Goodwill Games. That summer was rough. I had a problem with an armstand dive I was doing. A swimmer has to be able to pick his spots, in regard to where he is and where he needs to be, in the water. I was getting disoriented and seeing not the water, but the platform and the walls. I had no idea where I was in the air and no idea when to kick out, so I was wiping out badly. It was like I didn't know what I was doing.

My coach wasn't at that meet so I was on my own. It was a scary feeling because whenever I had needed confidence in the past all I had to do was look at my coach. That wasn't an option at the Goodwill Games. At that moment on the diving stand I decided, "I can't do this by myself. I will put everything aside. God, this is not in my hands, it is in Your hands. I trust You."

I didn't miss a dive the whole meet and I won the gold medal. I got up there to dive, still not seeing my spots, but believing in God. I felt taller, tighter, and stronger than ever before. I knew I was no longer alone. I have to thank diving for helping me look to God and realize He is there for me, not just in diving, but in everything I do. I had struggled with my faith before. I was raised a Christian and had been baptized, but it hadn't all come together until that day at the Goodwill Games.

God has given me these great gifts of determination and passion for something I love to do. I realized I had to give back to Him, to give God a product worthy of the gifts He has given me. I started putting everything into my workouts and daily life, because I realize now what I am working for. I love diving more than ever.

It's strange to see that a sport can do something like that. I love to dive, I enjoy it, and I want to win, but that's not why I do it. It's to glorify God. When I am alone I know I am my best friend and worst enemy, but the difference now is I trust God enough to have the courage to push forward.

Being able to compete internationally, in competitions like the Goodwill Games, is incredible. I enjoy the nervousness and excitement of standing on the podium and watching the American flag being raised while the national anthem is played. At the Goodwill Games, it was thrilling to see the athletes. I stayed up until 2 a.m. in the hotel lobby just to watch track star Michael Johnson walk by.

I had to beat two Chinese women in order to win the gold. The win was a victory over all of my fears, and it was the first time I felt I was really with God. My parents were there, too, and of course winning the gold and having the flag raised meant so much. I always wondered what I would do if I won. Would I sing the national anthem, or just stand there? When I won, I could do nothing but cry, because so many circles had been closed, yet a new part of my life was just beginning because of my relationship with God.

I love seeing little kids at our meets. When I was a little gymnast, I remember going to watch the stars compete. I hung over the railing, looking at my superheroes. If I can be an inspiration to a kid and change a child's outlook for the better, that means everything to me. I want to help kids believe in themselves. Dreams do come true.

After the Goodwill Games, I was severely dehydrated so I had to wait 90 minutes for the drug testing. I came out of the arena and there was a little girl waiting for me.

"Hi, my daughter wanted to wait for you," her mother said. "We heard you hadn't left. My daughter just started diving."

That knocked my socks off, and to this day I wish I had gotten her address and phone number. This little girl waited long into the night for me. She was a shy, adorable little girl, standing there holding a pen and T-shirt. Everything I had worked for was standing in front of me in the form of this beautiful child. I signed the shirt for her and walked her to her car as we talked.

That little girl left with a smile on her face. To this day, the memory she left me with gives me a smile that just won't go away.

DUNCAN KENNEDY
LUGE

Name: Duncan Kennedy
Sport: Luge
Born: Dec. 20, 1967, Burlingame, California
Family: Mother, Betsy; Brothers, Carter and Ian
Resides: Lake Placid, New York
Trains: Lake Placid, New York
Coach: Wolfgang Schadler (Liechtenstein)

Accomplishments: Top singles racer in U.S. history with 21 international medals; three-time Olympian; finished second in the overall World Cup standings in 1991-92 and 1993-94 seasons; fourth in World Cup standings in 1996-97 (most recent competitive season)

Hobbies: Golf, snowboarding, surfing, skateboarding

Post-Olympic goals and plans: Coaching

By Duncan Kennedy

Leaving the event I had dedicated my life to—the luge—just prior to the 1998 Olympics in Nagano was one of the toughest decisions I ever made.

I thought I was on schedule for my best showing ever, but that changed in a heartbeat. The first sign of a problem appeared when I was 14. I woke in our family home in Lake Placid, New York, not feeling well. The next thing I knew, I was airlifted to a hospital to receive a spinal tap. It was scary, but we didn't really figure out at that time what was wrong. The symptoms went away, and I went back to being an active kid. The technology then wasn't what it is today, so my condition went undiagnosed for the most part.

In 1996, I was competing in the World Cup season final in Nagano. Right before my last run, I became very dizzy in the starting house at the top of the run. I thought, "What's going on?" I really needed the points, so I thought, "I've got to make this run."

It was a fairly brief episode of dizziness, so I didn't think about it too much—I was guessing that it was just an allergy. In the fall of 1997 at Nagano, it happened again. I thought, "Something is terribly wrong."

Around Christmas of 1997, the doctor told me, "You shouldn't sled anymore. We can't clear you." Things were up in the air. I thought to myself, "Well, it's been a good run, but that's it. Everything is over with." Still, I didn't know if the condition would get worse.

This time, something was wrong. There was bleeding from near the brain stem. The illness is a cavernous malformation on the brain. One of the arteries running up my neck is naturally enlarged, and it gets worse under heavy stress, mental or physical. Since birth I've had this condition; the veins or capillaries can't handle the load from this enlarged artery. So I've had these small bleeds, and to my understanding, it has created some scar tissue.

This particular episode occurred as a result of some horrific personal problems that led to, and exacerbated, my condition. But this time the symptoms didn't go away. I sat in my hotel room, growing very disoriented and, to be honest, rather frightened. I thought, "This is what happened when I was 14." I knew something was definitely wrong.

The doctors in Nagano were being cautious in giving me clearance to fly home. It was November 1997 when I returned to the U.S. to be poked, prodded, and tested. Doctors had a vague idea of what it might be, but some were still confused. It wasn't until the spring after the 1998 Olympics that I went to see a specialist in California. I was in Sacramento, and this doctor made sense out of all my symptoms. In fact, he had contributed to a book about this condition. Finally knowing was a huge relief to me.

The doctor in Sacramento told me later that while my condition is brought on by stress, those early guesses were incorrect—the jarring my head took going down the luge track did not bring this on. Even though he was encouraging me to stay active, I personally didn't know if I could go back to the luge.

I thought about snowboard racing. The doctors and my neurologist encouraged me to be active, so snowboarding was something I could do.

Very slowly the symptoms were getting better. It was scary and frustrating, and at times it still can be. There are some days that I can't do that much, but they are few and far between compared to how it was during the very frightening period.

I do have, to some degree, symptoms almost all the time. But sometimes they are very slight—so slight they're difficult to describe. When they really come on, I get more off-balance than dizzy. My brain really slows down and it's very hard to process information. Writing a check can be a challenge. That's on a bad day, and those days are rare.

When I stopped sledding on the luge, I went right into snowboarding and went to Hobie Snowboards. They were developing new ideas and technology, and I thought, "This is neat. These guys are innovators." I helped them develop their race boards. They supplied me with boards for the season.

I started snowboarding, and I saw that I would never reach a high level of competition. Not because of the illness, but for one simple fact: I was not at a competitive level in terms of my skills.

It's frustrating because I am a pretty good snowboarder; I just didn't have the time to put into it to become world class. But for Hobie to give me a break was above and beyond what I could have hoped for, and I remain grateful to them. I was able to race the Eastern Series and I still stay involved a little bit with the snowboard programs. It's a great sport.

The symptoms from my illness subsided significantly. In 1999, I decided, "It's time to go slide."

So I was back in the luge. At the time I wasn't really looking for a competitive luge, I just wanted to slide recreationally while I was coaching. So with the snowboarding, coaching, and sliding I was able to stay active.

Then, something strange happened: I recorded my fastest time ever on the luge at Lake Placid. I went 37.9 seconds and I had never broken the 38-second barrier. I felt so at home on the sled. I thought, "Maybe...maybe I'm not done yet."

The times were so good I thought, "Maybe I should do this. Maybe I should race the World Championships." The 1999 Luge World Championships were on a track in Germany, one I am so familiar with I consider it a "home" track. But logistically, it didn't work out. In the spring of 1999, I did a spring cleaning of my head and re-evaluated everything. I put what happened into perspective.

I had been feeling much better. I had gotten into coaching. At the same time, the moment had come for me to get back on the sled.

I have always been a firm believer that it's great to take a day to go watch and listen. I've had several long breaks throughout my career. Back in 1990 I had almost a year off, and I didn't want to look at a sled until the next year.

In 1999, I realize the luge is in my blood.

If nothing else, this experience has been the most humbling of my career. It was an honor to participate in three Olympics (1988, 1992, and 1994). I am blessed to be a part of helping USA Luge grow.

It was never my goal to be considered the best American luge athlete ever—I wanted to be the best in the world. To tell you the truth, when I left the sport I wanted the other guys to kick my behind all over the place. Of course, now that I'm back, I want to kick them all over the place. Honestly, it's been really nice being near the forefront of the sport in this country. But I know I can only do it for so long.

My training is going real well. Physically, I plan on being in the best shape of my career for the upcoming season. However, in light of what I have gone through, I take it year by year, month by month, day by day. I really must at this point. In all honesty, I don't know what will happen. I mean, I don't think my symptoms will come back, but I never know.

I would love to have that Olympic medal around my neck. That, and the overall World Cup title is all I've ever wanted. I missed it by one point on two different occasions. I've been second in the overall World Cup point standings twice and third once. In the Olympics, I've had the worst luck. The year I was leading the World Cup (1991-92) all season, I was tenth in the 1992 Olympics. I had been winning races and been on the podium all year, but it just didn't happen at the Olympics.

Some of my friends and competitors think I'm unlucky because of the injury. My view is just the opposite. In a lot of ways, I'm the luckiest guy in the world, just to do what I've been doing. I wouldn't trade everything the sport has given me and everything I've given the sport for anything in the world.

As I mentioned, the injury also led me to coach. I truly enjoy that. Actually, I love coaching. I have strong relationships with the athletes, especially having been one in this sport for long. I learned a lot. I know that there's nothing worse than a coach who is condescending, one who puts himself or herself on a pedestal above the athlete. That's the worst thing to do, especially with the kids. At the younger levels, it does not create a healthy learning environment.

I've also learned a ton about myself through coaching. It's actually helped my sliding. In early 1999, I was telling the kids how to do something on the sled. I had already been through a couple of runs so I could demonstrate. I got on the sled and thought, "I have to do this right."

The Olympic pressure is nothing compared to this—the real pressure is when I tell kids how to do it, and then I have to show them. They were waiting to see if I could turn my words into actions.

Certainly that day I was teaching the development luge team was not the Olympics. But it embodied everything the Olympic spirit is about—paying attention, pushing myself, learning from mistakes, and having confidence.

When the kids I'm teaching learn something and then push through the challenges and master it, well, that's my Olympic memory, and to me, it's pure gold.

There is a postscript that seems to follow me wherever I go. It's been told and retold in the media, but this is the first time the whole, accurate story will be told.

Something happened in the fall of 1993 while we were training in Germany that opened my eyes to the face of hatred.

It was the birthday of U.S. doubles rider Chris Thorpe. We were in a bar having a beer and a skinhead came in with a T-shirt that read, "White Power."

With us was Robert Pipkins, the only black guy on the team. The guy in the T-shirt came over and made a gesture as he flaunted his shirt toward Robert. We were like, "OK, whatever. Have a good night."

But I knew how those guys worked. The few skinheads there at that time were just the tip of the iceberg, and no one else caught on that we were the *Titanic.* These two paths would cross soon, and there would be a disaster.

The skinheads sitting there wanted to provoke us. If they succeeded, very likely a bunch of their friends would come in when they heard a fight break out.

"Hey guys," I said to my friends, "Maybe we should finish our beers and just head out."

We stood up and got ready to go. At that point, 15 skinheads came marching in the door. It was the scariest thing I could ever imagine. They were making monkey sounds and racial slurs toward Rob. I hustled everyone out the door. I shoved Rob first and told him, "Run as fast as you can back to the hotel." I knew they were after Rob, but I didn't know if they would come after me. Rob was my friend, and we had to get him out first. I shuffled my other friends out and I exited last.

I tried to stall to give my friends time to get out of there. The bar was in a sunken-in area, so a couple hundred yards away was a long series of stairs that led up to the street. Rob had to get that far to have a chance to escape to safety. I made it to the stairs and saw everyone else had, also. I thought to myself, "Mission accomplished."

Or was it? Just a breath or two after I thought I was safe, the skinheads came running up the stairs. I needed to give Rob some more time, I thought. I stopped and put my arm down.

"Listen, you guys," I said, "you win. My friend left, and you got what you wanted. Let it go."

They formed a circle around me and beat me. I was knocked to the ground a few times. That wasn't good because they kicked me with those boots. I got up and threw a few punches in on one of the guys. That just made it worse. I almost got out of the circle a few times, but I was thrown in and knocked back down. On what I felt was my last chance, one or two of them must have let up because I was able to get out of there. I ran back toward the hotel.

My friends knew I had been left behind, so they had started coming back for me—they met me about halfway to the hotel. I was spitting up blood and bleeding from various parts of my face. My nose was broken, too. We called the police from the hotel.

"We can come out tomorrow," the policeman said on the phone.

My coach said, "You will come out now!"

The police came to the hotel. I gave them information and they said that wasn't good enough.

"You have to come down to the bar and identify all the men who you claim attacked you or we won't arrest them," the policeman said.

We headed to the bar—I knew this was probably how the skinheads escaped responsibility for their attacks, because the victims would never return to the scene of the crime for fear of further retribution. I knew I couldn't change the face of racism, but I wanted to give it a serious slap.

I thought the skinheads would have left the bar by then because they thought the police were coming. I was wrong. When we arrived at the bar there were dozens of skinheads outside. It was unbelievable. They all look alike—the shaved heads, green bomber jackets, and black boots.

When I got out of the police van, I picked a few of them out. I got into yelling matches with a couple of them. We went into the bar and they were just swarming. I recognized one of the instigators, the guy with the "White Power" T-shirt. He was leaning on the table with his head down and his buddies were surrounding him, trying to hide him.

I told the cops, "He's one of the ones who started it and kicked me."

The cop said, "You have to point to him."

"Listen, it's the guy with his head on the table," I said. "I don't have to point to him. You can tell who he is—right there."

"It's a legal thing," the cop said. "You have to point to him and say, 'That's him. That's the guy who assaulted me.'"

"Are you insane?" I asked him. "This guy has 35 of his drunk buddies in here."

"Point," the cop said, "or we do nothing."

"All right," I said. "But first you get at least five police officers around me."

The cops formed a shield around me.

"That's him!" I said, pointing directly to the "White Power" guy.

The place just exploded. The skinheads started fighting the police. A couple of the cops pushed me out the door and locked me in the police van for my safety.

I guess a few of the skinheads were arrested, though I don't know what happened to them or if they spent time in jail. I still get recognized for that event. It was very flattering to be labeled a hero by the press, but the thing that stinks is that this stuff happens all the time. The only reason this got media coverage was because I was an American athlete. I can tell you right now that in that German town—and in other countries all over the world, including ours—a black, Hispanic, or other minority is being assaulted, verbally or physically. Somewhere at this moment, a black's grave is being desecrated because of the color of his or her skin.

I feel privileged to be known for standing up for a racial issue—I only did the right thing. What I hope comes of this is that one less racial slur is made. Racism must become a zero-tolerance issue in this country, and in the world, and if I wear a label promoting racial harmony for that one small act, I wear it very proudly.

BELA KAROLYI
GYMNASTICS COACH

Name: Bela Karolyi
Sport: Gymnastics Coach
Born: Sept. 13, 1942, Cluj, Romania
Family: Wife, Marta; Daughter, Andrea
Resides: Houston, Texas
Athletes coached: Nadia Comaneci, Mary Lou Retton, Julianne McNamara, Phoebe Mills, Kim Zmeskal, Betty Okino, Kerri Strug, Dominique Moceanu

Accomplishments: In three decades of coaching produced 28 Olympians, nine Olympic champions, 15 world champions and 12 European champions; 1991 team silver medal at world championships (the first team medal the U.S. ever won in world championship competition); 1992 Kim Zmeskal won the all-around title (the first won by an American at the worlds); 1992 Olympics, U.S. captured its first medal in eight years—the team bronze was the first since 1948 that the U.S. won in a non-boycotted Olympics. Came out of retirement in 1996 to assist Zmeskal's comeback, and also coach Dominique Moceanu and Kerri Strug, who would go on to help win team gold in 1996 Olympics

Other interests: Running gymnastics business on my ranch in Houston; wrote life story, *Feel No Fear*

By Bela Karolyi

Coaching was not my first career choice. I was a physical education teacher in my younger adult life.

Teaching was instrumental in making me into the kind of coach I became over the years. In teaching physical education, one important objective is to help teach kids the confidence and awareness of their physical and mental development.

In 1960 I started teaching and coaching at the same time. I immediately translated everything from the general purpose of teaching to my coaching.

I felt all along that the sport was nice. But there was an obligation to not just teach physical skills, but to help enhance and stress the importance of a complete and well-rounded education.

Those days were long ago, but they were the foundation upon which my coaching career and life were built.

The satisfaction is seeing the young people develop into young adults. The medals or high placings are a bonus, but it's what happens to the individuals in real life that determines your success as a coach and teacher.

I get so much pride in watching my athletes grow. I love to see them smiling and happy while they are learning. I can say these people get so much from sports. It cannot be credited to the coach, because sports give young people a great chance to develop an attitude and confidence that will help them in life. These young people face obstacles every day. If they can learn something in the gym and get past those obstacles, they can apply those lessons to life.

They have to put in the effort to get the success. They realize goals and sometimes dreams because of their determination and commitment. That is a truly beautiful thing that sport offers to anyone.

Not long ago, Mary Lou Retton's second daughter was born. We got together and had just the greatest time. Seeing Mary Lou with her kids made my heart feel warm. It's great to see this woman whom I coached as a young person, and see what a wonderful mother she is. She still loves working with kids, and that produces such a positive effect on them.

I love to have the opportunity to chat and visit with my former athletes. I like to hear about their lives, the challenges they face, and how they overcome those challenges.

In 1996 I stepped out of national-level coaching and went full time doing what I love; working with the younger kids. That is where my passion and drive as a coach and teacher always rested. Five of my former athletes brought their daughters to my school. I had the greatest time seeing their uniqueness, but in some ways they are carbon copies of their mothers. It was hilarious and heart-warming.

It gives me the most satisfaction to see those people get to the point where they can lean on what they learned as athletes. They no longer compete in gymnastics, but they carry a reward for the rest of their lives from the hard work and instruction they went through. And I see the same love of life in their children—the same that their mothers had. That is an incredible thing.

Even when we were having our Olympic successes, we never considered our ultimate goal to be growing one beautiful flower. No, in the 36 years of coaching we always focused on all the kids, and the ones coming up. When we started in Romania with Nadia Comaneci's group we were still looking at the next gymnast. You have to look ahead for your program, or you will have to start from scratch if you have just one flower and ignore the seedlings.

When I think of the high performance required to create a champion, it is frustrating and dangerous in many respects. Because if I am not succeeding, I tend to consider my career over and unfulfilled, and all of my effort and time wasted. The important thing is to enjoy the process and learn the entire way. We want the kids to grow up to be healthy and strong. Not every Olympian is successful, and not every gymnast makes the Olympics. But for me, the pride was the same no matter what level the athletes reached, as long as they were the best they could be.

That again comes from my basic mission of teaching. I'm teaching them for their lives, not just for high athletic performance, though that was also an objective. They have to be prepared for their lives. Sports is a small part, just one sequence they will face through the decades.

My wife, Marta, the Olympic coach in 1996, has been a key to my success. I have to tell you without hesitation that from the beginning we were close in turning our dreams and goals into a live, tangible process. We shared the same type of goals with our team. We were all closely knit, hand-to-hand and shoulder-to-shoulder. We were able to share our successes together with the team we started with in America. Marta's contribution couldn't have been more beautifully outlined than when she had the honor and responsibility of coaching the team in the 1996 Olympics.

Marta and I defected in 1981 during an exhibition tour in the United States. When I first came to America, I knew one thing: I would not step into the scene and just line up with the mediocrity of where the sport used to be. I knew the American kids were just as good and powerful as the Romanians or Russians. It was just a matter of showing them the light, taking their hands and leading them for quality performances—and then shaking their hands when they reached their dreams. I knew they would neither stop nor run away. It was a gorgeous experience, just amazing.

Many people thought, "Oh, the Karolyis will just do a big splash here." They said, "Our kids have the highest standard of living but our kids are kind of lazy and don't want to go to the level of effort required to reach the top rung. They won't go hard for the high quality like the eastern Europeans did." That attitude was frustrating to me. I wasn't frightened, but it was hard to deal with those kinds of comments. Those statements did more to damage the kids than anything else. How does it make kids feel to hear someone say they are lousy, they are spoiled or they don't want to work? It was so disheartening to hear the awful tone of it.

From the moment we first stepped into a U.S. gym as coaches, I saw the same enthusiasm and the same smiles as those I had left behind. I thought, "Everything I've heard and read is a bunch of crud. These kids can do it."

When we first came to America, it was a time of hardship and sorrow, leaving Romania and what I had there. We had to start from scratch. But once I got into coaching here and saw the look in the kids' eyes, I felt their excitement. I could tell immediately the kids had faith in me. I told my wife, "Yes, we can do it. There is no doubt in my mind."

Leaving Romania was a hard decision; it wasn't based on a long talk or a well-prepared series of moves. I had to quickly make a decision based on inside pressure from the Romanian government pushing me to stay with their sports program. It wasn't an easy thing to do. With time, I was able to realize I have the power inside me to fight through the difficulties of starting over, working menial jobs until I was able to get into coaching again.

I came here by my choice and I believed I could start my life over again. This is the place where I wanted to spend the rest of my life. It was a choice that came from my heart with complete conviction. Never would I turn back or look back. I would not betray the mission I have here to help little kids. I would never leave America. This is a place where I once felt like a stranger, and now I cannot imagine living anywhere else. That I might have made a little contribution of making this sport more visible and popular is a great feeling as well.

One of the more gratifying and rewarding feelings has been to have our work appreciated. It was the ultimate when we could see our kids arrive on top of the world. I was so proud.

That draws everything back to the fact that this is my profession, my hobby, my conviction, and my life. People have sometimes been more interested in hearing me talk about things other than gymnastics. My message is always making sure they understand the sport is beautiful and that all sports can have a big impact on children's lives. The development makes them stronger, happier, and able to work within a team, and that helps them long into life.

Part of the reality is that these kids won't be at the top for an extensive period of time. That can be so wrongly understood. They can't step in and say, "I'm here to be an Olympic champion." That is not the purpose of sport. Indeed, sport can offer an athlete of any ability a great deal of experience. I am proud of the ones who end up with medals around their necks. But I am just as proud of the ones who worked hard and fought to reach their potential. That's something both the kids and parents have to understand.

NANCY SCHULTZ AMATEUR WRESTLING ADMINISTRATION

Name: Nancy Schultz
Sport: Amateur Wrestling Administration and Promotion
Born: June 5, 1959, East St. Louis, Illinois
Family: Widow of World and Olympic Champion David Schultz; Son, Alexander; Daughter, Danielle
Resides: Foster City, California
Schultz Club Athletes: Olympians: Kurt Angle, Dan Henderson: World Championship Team Members: Cary Kolat, Steven Neal, Eric Akin, Sandy Bacher, John Giura

Dave's accomplishments: A loving father of two; Olympic champion (1984); world champion (1983); five-time World Cup champion (1980, 1982, 1985, 1994, 1995); two-time Pan American champion (1977, 1987); Goodwill Games champion (1986) and silver medalist (1994); 10-time U.S. National champion; NCAA champion (1982); two-time Tblisi champion (1984, 1991); three-time world silver medalist (1985, 1987, 1993); two-time world bronze medalist (1982, 1986); three-time AAU national champion (1977 G-R, 1981, 1982 G-R); three-time NCAA All-American (1978, 1981, 1982); three-time DeGlane Challenge champion (1983, 1990, 1991); two-time Olympic Festival champion (1985, 1987); two-time Sunkist International champion (1989, 1990). U.S. records: First in most Tblisi Tournament titles; second in most world and Olympic medals; second in most world medals; second in consecutive world and Olympic medals; tied for second in most World Cup gold medals; tied for second in most World Cup medals; tied for fourth in most national freestyle medals

Nancy's accomplishments: Mother of two; president of the

Dave Schultz Wrestling Foundation; honorary co-chairperson of the "Wrestling for the Next Millennium" capital campaign; board member of USA Wrestling and the National Wrestling Hall of Fame; helped create the Dave Schultz High School Excellence Award and the Dave Schultz Memorial International Championship; 1997 *Wrestling USA Magazine* "Woman of the Year"; 1998 USA Wrestling's "Woman of the Year"

Nancy's hobbies: Traveling, watching wrestling, scuba diving, rock climbing, and sky diving

By Nancy Schultz

I am very surprised and honored when I hear people refer to me as a leader in this sport of wrestling. It is not because I chose this path, but more because it chose me.

David Schultz dedicated his life to sharing his extraordinary passion for amateur wrestling. He was a great athlete, a great ambassador, and a great friend to many. He was a positive person who taught me to draw strength from adversity.

When Dave was murdered, my world fell apart. I had two young children with no father and I found myself facing a court battle to bring justice to a defendant with almost unlimited resources. On Jan. 26, 1996, the day Dave was killed, my house was immediately filled with people offering their love and support. The children and I reaped the benefits from the kind of person Dave was and all the friendships and relationships he had developed around the world. He would have been so proud of his friends. The wrestlers were there, like a family, taking me to meetings with police, accompanying me to the morgue, and helping us move off the duPont estate. They helped me with every facet of my life after the murder. They sat beside me during the trial and gave me their support and strength.

Over the 15 years Dave and I were together, he was an athlete, leader, and coach, and I was somewhat of a den mother to many of the athletes, both U.S. and foreign. After Dave's death many of the athletes looked to me for some of the leadership Dave had shown them. There were about 20 athletes looking for a way to continue competing and training but who had wanted to break free from duPont's funding. At the same time many people throughout the wrestling community were contacting me to see how they could help. I put the two groups together: athletes who needed help and individuals who wanted to help them.

Everyone wanted to help. USA Wrestling, our national governing body, helped in every way. The University of Pennsylvania and the YMCA donated places for the athletes to train. ASICS sponsored our equipment, and the United States Olympic Committee presented a $50,000 grant. Attorneys volunteered to help draft the paperwork to form a non-profit organization. Donations came in from around the world. Everything came together and the Dave Schultz Wrestling Foundation was formed.

The U.S. National Open was in March 1996. I kept hearing David's name called out during the tournament and yet he wasn't there. It was strange and sad, but at the same time I was happy because it was his legacy and spirit that created the motivation to push forward. The fact that it all came together surprised me, in that it happened so quickly. The Dave Schultz Wrestling Club took second in the U.S. We had a team and many athletes had competed successfully. I remember saying aloud, "Wow, Dave, it worked." I had to take some time and let it all sink in.

My background is in sports administration. I had worked with the city's park and recreation programs as well. I was familiar with the process of organizing teams, travel, and keeping the records. I also had many wonderful friendships throughout the wrestling community to rely on for advice and coaching help. It wasn't too much of a leap to handle the basics of running the business but it was definitely different being a woman administrating a national wrestling club. I was spread very thin and I'm still not sure how I came up with the time. The needs of our children were first during sad and challenging times, then the legal issues surrounding David's death, and then the club, which gave me the strength and support to handle all the rest.

Originally, I didn't really think of the Schultz Club as something long term, but was simply focused on getting Dave's teammates through the tryouts for the '96 Olympic Team. I didn't think much beyond that. If the guys made the team, USA Wrestling would sponsor them, and if they didn't there would be a break until the next competitive year. So I just had to make it until the U.S. Olympic Team trials in June.

The 1996 Atlanta Olympic games was an emotional event with many highs and lows. It was Alexander's (10) and Danielle's (7) first Olympics, but no father was there to proudly watch below. Good friends Kendall Cross, Kurt Angle, Tom Brands, Townsend Saunders and Bruce Baumgartner all received medals, but Dave was not there to share a high five and a hug. I saw all the friendly faces that I know so well, people from Iran, Turkey, Russia, Bulgaria, and Belarus, but instead of exuberant greetings with Schultzie as my translator, there were bowed heads and silent condolences. I could feel their compassion and sorrow. Loving embraces and words to honor Dave flowed freely in many different languages. Yes, it was painful but it was also one more step in the healing process for my children and me.

When the Olympics ended, the guys looked at me and said, "You're not getting out now!" It was great. No one wanted to quit. The coaches, the athletes, the trainers, the fans, everyone encouraged me to continue. I kept thinking, "What is my best option?" I decided to keep the kids around the familiar environment, the wrestling family. For it is there they can get the same kind of support and love they had when their dad was alive. It's a good place for them and for us.

People seemed to love David more than he knew. Even he would have been surprised. David was a generous and kind person. When he went to Russia he took medicine, food, and Bibles, and would reach and touch everyone he met. After his death people told me stories about David, about how he had interacted with them. The way people honored him surprised me. David has been portrayed as a public figure but his interactions with people were very personal. We live in a hectic age and pass through people's lives without stopping, but David wasn't like that. The president of USA Wrestling said David was a man with 10,000 best friends. David built that, one friendship at a time. I felt that too. I wasn't just his wife, but also his friend.

Dave found his passion for the sport of wrestling in junior high school. His dyslexia led a teacher to suggest extra physical exercise. From the first moment he was introduced to a wrestling room, he knew that this was what he wanted to do for the rest of his life. I've heard stories of a young Dave riding an old bicycle, wearing his singlet (wrestling uniform) under his jeans, his wrestling shoes over the handlebars, ready to wrestle at a moment's notice.

He became accomplished at a young age and at 16 he was a successful international athlete. His career spanned 20 years. He learned to speak Russian so he could communicate with the people there as well as improve his wrestling technique. He interacted with many international athletes and political representatives. He enjoyed meeting people from other countries, and often those friends from around the world would come visit us. He filled our lives with richness and adventure.

David's father is a counselor and a spiritual man, a very sweet soul. When I first started dating David, I met his brother Mark (later to become an Olympic champion beside his brother). The three of us went to California to visit their father, Phil. Here were these two hulking wrestlers, yet when they walked into their father's house they were allowed to be children. They sat on the couch with their father, with their heads on his lap and he was patting the top of their heads. These two huge, muscular men turned into little mush balls around their father. They were tough guys but they had gentle sides.

Although David was very busy with wrestling, he always found a way to include his family. People would sometimes ask me if I was frustrated with the hectic pace of our lives, but there is a flexibility to the athlete's lifestyle and schedule if you take advantage of it. David could be home during the day and could take the kids to and from school.

David was a wonderful father. He started a bedtime story when

Xander was 2 years old, and continued this ongoing story to him and later to Danny until the day before he died. Our frequent visitors from around the world participated in these adventures, each becoming a character in the story for the evenings they were at our house.

Sometimes he ate lunch at the elementary school cafeteria. The principal recently reminded me of a time when Dave volunteered, "Ice cream for everyone!" In the ensuing mayhem, he paid for the whole school to have a round of ice cream. The principal called me and said, "Your big kid is at the school. Are you coming to get him?" He was a popular character with the kids and staff.

When Alexander was 4 years old, David was invited to share his Olympic medal with the preschool class. "Your teachers asked me to come here to speak today because I won an Olympic medal. If you get really good at playing games you can win one, too." His message to young people has always been, "Find something you love, whether music, art, sports or whatever. When you find something you are passionate about, then you can achieve greatness."

On the mat, Dave was more than just a competitor. He really loved the art of wrestling and has been called the Einstein of wrestling. He was a perfectionist at his art. Some wrestlers have to get mad at their opponents to get fired up, but not David. He wanted to be the best wrestler possible. It didn't have much to do with who was standing on the other side of the mat. The higher the quality of his opponent, the more excited David became. Watching him wrestle was like an artful dance, almost a ballet of wrestling. Sure, he was quite strong, but it wasn't brute strength that got him to that level. He was clean and exact with his technique.

One year in the finals of the world championships, Dave faced Adlan Variev from Russia. David went to the center of the mat with this huge smile on his face. He slapped Adlan's hand and said, "It's time to play." This competition is as tough as it gets—one world champ against the other. Yet Adlan had just carried our sleeping son to the tournament site from the hotel. They were good friends as well as competitors. They respected each other.

I have a huge hole in my life; I miss Dave every day. Never does a day pass that I don't think about the impact of this horrible tragedy on our children. I want them to be able to hold onto David and remember him. He had so much to offer them in so many ways. He had wisdom and a quest to live life to its fullest every single day. Our daughter struggles to remember him. She runs down the stairs and says she can't remember what her father looked like or sounded like. I tell her about him and we watch a video. It frightens me that the memory of her father is fading. I had many years with David and they had so few.

There are many concerns in our life—financial, legal, and emotional. And so now I surround myself with the world of amateur wrestling. I use David's loving memory, his leadership, and his devotion to wrestling as a source of inspiration to build the Dave Schultz Wrestling Foundation. Through this foundation I will continue in his footsteps to encourage, promote, and support amateur wrestling in the United States. I serve on the board of USA Wrestling, the Board of Governors for the National Wrestling Hall of Fame, and I am co-chair of a capital campaign to raise money for our future Olympians.

The DSWF is a national non-profit organization with regional affiliate training sites throughout the United States. We raise approximately $50,000 each year. This pays for partial competitive expenses, including travel, and room and board for our athletes placing in the top six in the U.S. We currently have four athletes competing in the world championships. We hope to put four to six athletes on the U.S. Olympic team in Sydney.

It has not been easy. I have had to be strong when I wanted to cry; I have grieved in front of millions when I wanted to be strong, but it is because I want to make a difference. David taught me to love this sport of amateur wrestling that is so misunderstood and so overlooked. It is a beautiful, technical sport that teaches dedication, discipline, and self respect, and then gives back to our society a group of outstanding Americans who go on to accomplish great things in our country. It is a sport that welcomes those from all walks of life. But mostly, it is a family. It is my family—the family that has carried Alexander, Danielle, and me through the most difficult time in our lives. I will continue to enter the auditoriums with all the sights and sounds that are so familiar to me and take comfort in the arms of wrestling. David taught me the medals will come and go, but the friendships, life's true treasures, will last forever.

LENNY KRAYZELBURG
SWIMMING

Name: Lenny Krayzelburg
Sport: Swimming
Born: Sept. 28, 1975,Odessa, Russia
Family: Father, Oleg; Mother, Yelena
Resides: Los Angeles, California
Current Coach: Mark Schubert

Accomplishments: Set three world records at 1999 Pan Pacific champions, 50-meter backstroke (24.99), 100-meter backstroke (53.60), 200-meter backstroke (1:55.87). American record holder in 200-meter backstroke; 1999 U.S. summer nationals, first place in 100- and 200-meter backstroke; 1999 U.S. Spring Nationals, first place in 100- and 200-meter backstroke; 1998 world championships, gold medal (100-, 200-meter backstroke), silver medal (400 medley relay); 1998 Goodwill Games, first place (200-meter back stroke), second place (100-meter back stroke); 1998 national champion, (100-, 200-meter backstroke)

Hobbies: Listening to classical and Italian music, reading business publications, learning about the stock markets, being with friends

Post-Olympic goals and plans: Continue swimming, explore other opportunities

By Lenny Krayzelburg

It was by chance that my family and I were able to leave Odessa, Russia, and come to America in late 1989.

We were fortunate because there was no rhyme or reason to the system of letting people leave. It was very arbitrary.

I was 13 years old when we left, and while I was an above-average swimmer, there was no idea that I would become a world-class swimmer.

Our family had a pretty good life in Russia. Our salaries were definitely above average, so life wasn't very tough for us. I have heard stories about people who could not get food and who had terrible lives, but it just wasn't like that for us.

My parents moved to the United States because they did not see a future in Ukraine for their children. I was excited to leave and was so young I didn't know the challenges I'd face. All I knew was that I had been told America was the best country in the world and that's where we were headed. Now, as I look back, it's funny to even believe I didn't know what might lie ahead. And I know now that it was a tough decision for my parents to leave Russia. They were taking us to an unknown area, not knowing what would happen.

When we came to Los Angeles, the toughest part for me was the language. Sure, I had had English in school, but English classes in another country are like vocabulary lessons only. What helped me in Los Angeles is that there was a pretty big Russian community. I was in junior high and there were a lot of Russian kids my age, including many that had come to the United States when I did.

That made the transition much easier. I was able to make new friends, and some were Russian. I could talk with them in my language and we could discuss the challenges we faced.

Only two weeks after coming here, I joined a swim team. My father didn't want to waste any time. He always liked me swimming. Even when we were emigrating, (we were in Austria and Italy during the process for a couple of months), he had me do dry land training.

Early on, I made friends in Los Angeles through swimming—it really helped me with my English. I like to meet different people, and everyone was so open-hearted. Since I was from Russia, everyone wanted to find out about how life was there.

Even now people think Russia is a poor country where people barely survive, but it's not that way for everyone. Look at the United States: There are people dying of starvation and homeless people.

Russia does have a lower standard of living, but it is a great country. Russia is a country that is very oriented toward family, more so than here. The divorce rate here is much higher. That's why when I marry it will be a Russian woman, because I want to keep my heritage a big part of me.

I don't think a person should ever forget where he came from. There are so many important things we learn at such a young age. Our whole personality develops while we are young. I did that in Russia—no one can take that away. I'm always going to treasure that. My heart is close to Russian people and American people. But Russia is where I was born. That's how I look at it. Here I have a lot of Russian fans. At home I speak Russian. I still have a lot of support in Russia.

Things in Russia are always overblown in the media. I went back in the summer of 1998 and I thought things were better than when I left. It's definitely a lot more westernized. It will open up to be a democratic country sooner or later. There are a lot of problems right now. But it is hard to change what 75 years of communism did in 10 years. It takes time and patience. Generations have to change. There are still some people controlling the country now who were part of the communist government. So a lot can happen, and it's unpredictable.

My father watches Russian television via satellite every day. He is so mind-boggled by what is going on and it's something different every day. When a whole generation turns over, and the young people take over the country, it will become more democratic.

As a teenager, I found that people in California were just great to me, and that made the transition easy. All of the parents of the kids on the swim team were great. They took me to the meets and brought me home because my parents couldn't.

I swam for the Jewish Community Swim Club. The second semester of my senior year of high school I sent out letters to colleges. No one answered. So I signed up at Santa Monica City College for classes for the fall. I talked to the swim coach and told him I was coming to school. I told him my times and he was impressed, because my times were above average for junior college. I was still in high school but he let me start training with his team.

That's when my career really took off. It was probably the first time in my life that the people I was swimming with were better than I was. I like challenges and seeing people better than me made me work harder. That's part of the reason I got better.

After my freshman year at Santa Monica, my coach, Stu Blumkin, felt I could swim at the Division I level. He talked to Mark Schubert at the University of Southern California in the summer of 1994 and asked if I could train with his team.

"That's fine," Mark said. "We're here for the community and if someone wants to train and is able to be competitive, that's fine. We'll be glad to give him a chance."

I was still working full time to help my parents and support myself. In the water, Mark saw my potential. By the end of the summer, I got my associate's degree.

For five years I was swimming just to stay in shape. Because of my situation with citizenship, my family, work, and everything else, I didn't have the ideal situation to train. I didn't have long-term goals. I just took advantage of what was available. Never in my wildest dreams did I think I'd reach the level I'm at now. So becoming a student-athlete at USC starting my sophomore season was a big turning point for me.

In 1995, I finally got American citizenship. That was important, because for five years I was caught between countries. Becoming an American citizen was a special moment for me, and I knew this was the country for me from that point on. Knowing I might be able to represent the U.S. in world or Olympic competition is a huge honor. Everyone around the world wants to beat the United States, so to be a part of holding off those challenges means a lot to me.

But I still had a lot of work to do when I got to USC in 1995. Everyone was better than I was. I walked into the pool the first day and I couldn't believe how big everyone was. It was very intimidating at first. We swam five hours a day, and I hadn't done that before. Even though everyone was better, I could compete.

I was so glad to have the opportunity to train with those people. Each day I took advantage of it. I worked harder every day. Even now I take advantage of every single day of practice. If I am going to be there every day, I might as well give 100 percent. There is no point just doing laps for hours and hours. I have to get something out of it. If I'm doing something I want to give 100 percent.

I was training with Brad Bridgewater, and I saw him win at the Olympics. My coaches at USC told me, "Lenny, you are good enough to be the best backstroker in the world." Mark Schubert had coached many world record holders and Olympians, so it meant a lot that someone like that could see something special in me.

I had been training and swimming with a lot of confidence, but got sick right before the NCAAs in 1996. So it was a tough year.

At the Olympic Trials in 1996, I was seeded second going into a finals. I was young and inexperienced and it was only my third competition in terms of swimming a long course. I was a raw rookie. It was disappointing. But I was two seconds faster than my previous best time. That's all I could ask for. In our sport it's difficult to compare yourself to someone else. I can only control what I do, not what the guys next to me do. I didn't think I was ready to be an Olympian. I really haven't thought about not making the 1996 team. I don't like to live in the past because I can't bring it back. I don't think, "If I'd only done this or that, or gone out a little faster, I'd have made the Olympic team."

I only live for today and tomorrow, not yesterday. It was a confidence builder just to know I belonged at this level and I could compete with those guys after only training at USC for five months.

I told Mark, "I will win nationals this summer." I was training full time and won summer nationals. From there on my confidence built and everything snowballed.

I kept working and training with Brad and realized my potential. In the summer of 1997 when I first broke the 200-meter backstroke record, everyone around me expected me to do it. It's a great honor, but it's not my ultimate goal. I don't think I'll be satisfied with my swimming career unless I win a gold medal at the Olympics. Having the records is an honor, but nothing close to what Olympic gold would mean.

I know that whatever I do, I can be successful. I do have a natural talent to be a swimmer, but more importantly I have the work ethic. That sounds like bragging, but it really isn't. I just don't mind working hard or staying after practice if that's what it takes to be the best. Hard work isn't a big deal to me. Some people are afraid of the pain training hard brings, but I welcome it.

I learned my work ethic from my parents. I'm a big sports fan, too. I have seen great athletes and their drive to be the best. I read about great athletes and see their characteristics. So much heart and soul goes into this sport, and I want to be the best, and I feel like I can be the best.

I am in the right country to reach my goals and excel. If I am successful, I have a greater opportunity to be someone here. In this country, hard work in sports is a springboard to the real world, which is competitive. I don't know that I'd have that opportunity in Russia. I will never forget Russia and that it is a great country, but the level of opportunity is just not there. Kids who are born in the United States don't realize the many opportunities they have.

It's an honor to be an American and I'm proud to represent this country.

JILL NEWMAN
TRIATHLON

Name: Jill Newman
Sport: Triathlon
Born: June 8, 1968, Rochester, Minnesota
Family: Husband, Dane Chalmers
Resides: Colorado Springs, Colorado
Trains: Colorado Springs, Colorado; San Diego, California
Coach: Dane Chalmers

Accomplishments: Juris Doctorate Degree (Law), University of California, Davis (1994); chairperson of International Triathlon Union Athlete's Committee; member of USA Triathlon's Athlete's Advisory Counsel. Multi-sport honors: Pan Am Games team qualifier for 1999; selected to USA Triathlon national "gold" team for 1999. Triathlon: first place (elite) 1999 La Serena (Chile) "Top 15" International Triathlon; second place (elite) 1999 Pucon (Chile) International Triathlon; second (elite) 1999 Antofogasta (Chile) International Triathlon: second (elite) 1999 St. Anthony's Triathlon and Pan Am Games qualifier, and Pan Am Games team qualifier

Hobbies: Reading, anything athletic, helping husband remodel home

Post-Olympic goals and plans: Have children, resume legal career

By Jill Newman

My life has had so many unlikely turns, from a childhood where I was active in many sports, to law school and now, as a triathlete.

Growing up in San Diego, I remember from the time I was four years old listening to my great uncle talk about his athletic career. Uncle Fred—Fred Feary—won the bronze medal in heavyweight boxing at the 1932 Olympics in Los Angeles. I loved listening to his stories, and did so through high school and college. I was a runner and he offered me a lot of coaching advice.

Uncle Fred told stories about fighting and boxing. He was a fighter during rather meager times and to him it was really important to represent the United States in the Olympics. He learned life's lessons and values through sports. He was a tough person in a tough sport, and he was a tremendous inspiration to me. I used to love to look at his medals and listen to him.

He always had some funny training tips, like eating steaks before a big competition, and consuming raw eggs for extra protein—things that seem a little antiquated. He also told me about "belly breathing" and explained, "That's why I never got a gut!" He was a great man who loved sports—all sports—and he always really encouraged us to participate. He died in 1995 so he never got to see me compete at the world-class level in triathlon. But I think of Uncle Fred often.

I have been a runner since I was 11 years old. I had some success and ran in college at the University of California-Davis, a good Division II school. I was better at playing soccer when I was growing up, but when I entered college there were more options in the sport of running, so it was my choice.

When I graduated from UC-Davis in 1991, I entered road races because I wanted to continue running. I usually placed around fourth and I knew I would never be much better than that. I sometimes wondered, "Why am I running road races?" because I was often frustrated with my performance. I didn't know much about triathlons and had only seen the Ironman triathlons on television. I thought, "These people are crazy—all these guys running around for a whole day in their Speedos." It seemed like such a strange sport.

I started law school in 1992 and was looking for something athletically challenging. Before law school, I worked as an ocean lifeguard in San Diego during the summers of 1988-1992. Many of the lifeguards were triathletes. During my last summer I entered my first triathlon where I placed second. My great love for the sport emerged after that first race.

After graduating from law school, I began working as a business attorney at a prestigious law firm in Newport Beach, California. At times I worked 80 hours a week, and though my training was sporadic, it was intense. Dane Chalmers, my fiancé at the time, trained me and was my support system as well.

While working in 1996, I won the age group national championships and placed fourth at the Escape from Alcatraz Triathlon where I found myself ahead of some very good professional triathletes. In the back of my mind I thought, "What if I gave triathlon a serious go? How could I do?" However, I had just started my law career and quitting to become a full-time triathlete was a difficult decision to make.

Then in the spring of 1996, I was asked by USA Triathlon, our sport's governing body, to join the U.S. Triathlon resident team at the Olympic Training Center in Colorado Springs where I would concentrate on making the 2000 Olympic team. Since U.S. Triathlon thought I had the ability to succeed as an elite triathlete, it made it easy to take a break from my career. I knew that this would be the only time in my life that I'd get a chance to train for the Olympic Games.

As an elite, I trained hard and raced well. By the end of 1997, I was ranked No. 13 in the world. In April 1998, I participated in a seven-mile race in San Diego and ran my personal record time.

The next day I took my parents' two dachshunds for a walk. Up to this point I had survived many grueling triathlons and training, but walking the dogs nearly ended my career.

There was a small incline in the sidewalk where the concrete had cracked. I tripped, fell forward and landed on my right hip. It was just a crack in the sidewalk—what a stupid thing to happen.

I got up and didn't really think about it. The next few days, however, my leg kicked out to the side when I walked. Still, I got on an airplane a few days later to participate in a World Cup race in Japan. When the plane landed, I got up but I couldn't walk correctly. At the time I didn't think it was the result of the fall.

In Japan, I tried to find a doctor or chiropractor—someone who could tell me why I couldn't run. I didn't have any luck so I raced anyway. That wasn't good. I ended up coming home in a wheelchair. X-rays and bone scans were done by the physicians at the Olympic Training Center in San Diego, and at first nothing showed up. Since the doctors ruled out a fracture, I started to rehabilitate an undiagnosed soft tissue injury.

Rehabilitation didn't work and the pain in my hip became more intense. This was devastating for me, and very frustrating for the sports trainers. I was spending four or five hours a day trying to rehabilitate my leg, but I couldn't balance. I couldn't stand on my leg. The doctors thought it might be neurological; they just couldn't figure it out. The physical therapists and doctors tried everything humanly possible to get me back in action.

I started running again on a treadmill. I could last just 10 minutes and even that was very painful and very awkward. I progressed on the treadmill for three days, and managed to run 16 or 17 minutes. I remember that time very vividly, because I was getting ready to get married. On the third day of training, I was so proud because I had gone for 18 minutes on the treadmill, my best performance by far. As it turned out, those three days only made it worse.

I had had a magnetic resonance imaging test earlier in the day, and the phone rang when I got home. It was the doctor.

"You have to come to my office right away," he said. "You have a broken hip. Don't run, and be careful when you walk. We don't want you to fall off a curb and break it all the way through."

As I was talking to the doctor, my fiancé was standing next to me. I grabbed a pen and pad and wrote, "Oh crap, broken hip." I was devastated.

But at least we finally knew what was wrong and had a diagnosis to work with. It was the worst injury I could have imagined, but we were no longer dealing with a mysterious problem.

This all occurred in May 1998 as I was doing the last-minute preparations for our wedding, making sure the flowers and cake were ready, and coordinating things for our 150 guests.

I made the wedding and am proud to say I made it down the aisle without crutches. But I had to alter the outfit. I wore white tennis shoes with nice, fancy bows during the reception.

To be honest, at that time of my life it was nice not to have to worry about training. I focused on the wedding and was able to spend some quality time with my husband.

When I started training, all I could do was swim and work out in the pool. I was not able to run for awhile because if my hip broke all the way through, I might have had to deal with avascular necrosis, the degenerative hip condition that Bo Jackson suffered from.

While I was anxious to train and speed the recovery so I could run, my bone needed rest. The minimum recovery time was supposed to be from 12 to 16 weeks. I was lucky in one respect—the hip broke from the bottom up. Had it cracked from the bottom down, it most likely would have broken all the way through.

I listened to the doctors and read all I could about the injury. Reading helped me come to terms with it really quickly—I knew I had to let my bone heal. If it didn't, my triathlon career would be over. Even if it did heal, I knew I had a lot of time before I could come back. I thought about returning to work and not focusing on triathlons.

"Let's take this time and work on your swim," my husband said, as swimming was my weakness. "Let's do something that will keep you involved in the sport and hopefully keep you going forward toward your Olympic goal."

With this, I was able to maintain my focus and not take a step back. It's frustrating to be an athlete who loves to train and to have it taken away.

The injury proved to be a blessing. It's strange to think that way, but it really was a blessing in disguise. Before the injury, in late 1997, I had improved tremendously and had made great gains. But holding onto a peak from 1997 all the way to the 2000 Games just wasn't realistic. The injury gave me some rest from the daily training and the mental rest that so few athletes take. An athlete would never schedule four months off—that's obscene for an athlete to even think about.

I came back with a new freshness. When something is taken away, we find out how much we enjoy it and how much it means to us. I consider every race I run to be a great gift—to participate in something I love. My setback made me realize my passion to train. It is not work, but something I truly enjoy. The injury was just something stupid that ended up being frustrating. But it also ended up being something very good—not that I want it to happen again.

Taking off most of 1998 helped me get my focus where it needed to be. It let me study myself as an athlete, let me realize where I was weak and allowed me to see where I could improve. I now have more direction than ever. However, I did miss a lot of training time, so when I train now I'm very focused—no fluff workouts or just messing around. To make up for lost time we've streamlined a lot of what I do. The competition continues to be fierce, and since the injury, my desire also has become fiercer.

I feel like I have something to prove when I race now. When I was out, I felt forgotten. I saw all my friends racing and thought, "Don't forget about me." Now I have this great need to prove myself again. I was gone for a year, but I'm back. I am a contender. I'm training and racing with more of a desire to improve—and prove—myself. I see athletes training sometimes who don't enjoy it—they think it's tedious. If these athletes experienced what I have, it might make them enjoy training more. An injury is a great way for an athlete to find himself. Training can become drudgery to any athlete. But I'll tell you this: Have it taken away for a short time. Take a step back, and you will discover your passion. It was great for me to learn that I was on the right track to pursue my goal.

Even with the injury, I've always thought of my life as being really enjoyable. I can't think about what I will be doing in the future, because the path I'm on always changes—for the better. There are struggles and tribulations in everyone's life; getting past the roadblocks leads us to better things. My mom always said, "I'm not worried about you. You do these things that don't seem logical, but you always land on your feet." And I always end up a better person for the experience.

I could have given up and said, "That's it, no more triathlon." But I didn't. Within a year of my injury, I qualified for the Pan Am Games, which was fantastic. However, I knew it wouldn't have been the end of my life if I hadn't made the U.S. team. I know that in my life, if I apply myself to something, I enjoy myself and I will be successful. If it's not fun and challenging, it's not worth doing.

When I came back so quickly, a few people thought I was a little crazy. Once I was cleared—the fracture fully healed—I raced a World Cup race three weeks later. The doctors and trainers only wanted me to run two or three times a week. Racing so quickly was stretching the guidelines they gave me. But I did the Clean Air Triathlon in early August 1998, after only running four times. I won the event, had a good swim and bike ride. I knew I couldn't rely on my run because I hadn't been running.

I raced a World Cup race in Canada two weeks later, toward the end of August. My competitors were more than surprised to see me.

"What are you doing?" one asked. "You are insane. You haven't trained!"

There was a good point in there, the level of competition is so extreme. But this time, I had no expectations, which was a different feeling than ever before. When I have no run training, I have no confidence. It was still important to compete because I can learn things from competition that I can't learn from training. It was a chance to test my improved swimming, and I could work on my transition and then go really hard on my bike. I could try new things and show my passion for being back.

I smiled more in that event than I've smiled my whole life. I raced knowing that I am so lucky.

Some of my friends currently have injuries and health problems, and I like to think that they can look to me for inspiration and say, "She did it—I can come back, too." I get letters and e-mails from athletes suffering from injuries, and it's so great to give advice. I know that being injured sometimes causes feelings of loneliness and stagnation. If I can help anyone get through adversity, I like to do it. You ask questions when you are injured: "Was that my only chance? Will I come back? What's my life going to be like?"

I have witnessed this firsthand. My sister, Jennifer Leck, was an Olympic-caliber figure skater. I was always "Jenny's little sister," and I loved that. She worked at her sport from a young age, through grade school and high school. She made tremendous sacrifices. I felt sorry for her sometimes, because I had so many interests, yet she only had time for figure skating. Jenny totally focused on one goal—the Olympics—and few people do that. She had always been a role model to me, and I admired the way she pursued skating. But that ended in 1987 when she suffered from compartment syndrome in her shins from the constant pounding and stress. She had surgery and her career ended, and yet she had no regrets.

So when we were getting ready for my wedding, she really perked me up. I saw that she succeeded in her life without skating. She is a kindergarten teacher now. She has children and she's married. The attributes she has are ones she had as an athlete, and she carried them off the ice and into life.

I am so proud of her.

While she heard the doctors talking to me before the wedding, she understood. The doctors said, "We hope you can recover. We hope the bone doesn't die." When I heard all of that negative stuff, I needed support. She knew the same thing that happened to her could be happening to me. The common experience of going through the severe injury brought us even closer.

So I knew I had her support, regardless. And my family, especially my husband, was there too. I also knew that whatever happened, it wouldn't be the end of my life.

Never in my wildest dreams did I think all this could happen—law school, switching careers, the success, the injuries, the support, the success again. I have a great husband and a great life. I couldn't be any happier.

UGUR TANER
SWIMMING

Name: Ugur Taner
Sport: Swimming
Born: June 20, 1974, Istanbul, Turkey
Family: Mother, Gulcin; Father, Erol
Resides: Tucson, Arizona
Hometown: Bellevue, Washington
Trains: University of Arizona
Current Coach: Frank Busch

Accomplishments: 1994, 1995, 1996 NCAA champion in 200-meter butterfly, eighth-fastest man ever in 200-meter butterfly, second fastest in U.S. history, two-time U.S. national champion; 1994 world championship gold medalist as a member of the 4x100m free relay; eighth-fastest American ever in the 200m freestyle; Pan Pacific Championship meet record holder in the 200m butterfly (1:57.35) as well as being a member of the 4x200m free relay (7:13.99); 1992 Olympian as a representative of Turkey

Hobbies: Reading, movie watching, bicycling, and playing guitar

Post-swimming: Plans on pursuing a career in modeling

By Ugur Taner

I was born in Istanbul, Turkey, and came to America when I was seven months old.

I always played in the pool in our community, but I didn't join the summer swimming club until I was nine years old. When I turned ten I joined a year-round team that had a one-workout-per-day program.

The more meets I participated in, the better I became. When I improved enough to best a rival who had been beating me, I moved up in age groups.

I was always climbing up the swimming ladder, and am still climbing, to this day.

I moved into the senior group when I was 13. The workouts were still once a day, but they were more intense. I was becoming a higher caliber swimmer. I had a breakthrough year when I was 14 by making the senior national.

I worked hard and set the national age group record for 13-14-year-olds in the 50 freestyle, the 100 free, 200 free, and the 200 intermediate medley.

I went up to the next level and was swimming with stars like Matt Biondi. I thought, "I'd like to make it to the national team." I looked at the times those swimmers were putting up, and thought, "Oh my gosh, I can't believe how fast that is!" I had done that the whole way through. When I was 10 or 11, I looked at the standards for junior nationals, and those times also seemed fast. But somehow, I made the cuts.

I made the national junior team when I was 17. We had a meet in Canada, and that was my first U.S. team experience.

I went back to Washington for my senior year of high school. I swam pretty well all through high school, but my senior year was the big one. I set national public high school records in the 50 and 100 freestyle, and the 100 butterfly. In my home state of Washington, I set the records in the 50, 100, and 200 freestyle, and the 100 butterfly.

That was a great way to finish high school. But I also had a goal of being the first high school student to break the 20-second barrier in the 50 free. I went 20.02 seconds, just barely missing it. That was a disappointment, but high school swimming was a lot of fun. And disappointments help a person to get better.

I started looking at colleges and received letters from all over. My parents and I narrowed the list to five schools. I wanted a good, competitive college program that had a good record, produced good swimmers, and had a good reputation. In this order, I took my five NCAA-allotted recruiting trips: UCLA, Tennessee, Michigan, Texas, and California. I enjoyed each trip more than the one before.

I suppose had the order been different, I might have ended up at another school. California was last and for some reason I enjoyed it the most.

I was still young when I was in college. I didn't know how to get myself to the next level on my own. I was immature and couldn't figure things out.

I won three NCAA championships in the 200 fly from 1994 to 1996. Actually, when I look back, I could have been a much better college swimmer. But things happen for a reason. I had a big turning point in my career at the 1996 Olympic Trials. A lot of my friends and teammates thought I was capable of making the Olympic team.

Being at the Olympic Trials is the most stressful competitive situation in the world. Swimming in the U.S. is very competitive. There are many good swimmers and there's a lot of depth. In other countries there are one or two guys who are fast and then there's a big drop-off. It's obvious who will be on the Olympic team for other countries, whereas in America we have people changing places year to year. Someone can make national team one year and not make it the next. There are people crying all over the place at the meet for the U.S. Olympic Trials. For a lot of people it's their only chance.

I don't like the amount of emphasis that is put on the Olympics. It is the pinnacle of sports, and while something has to be, some people feel like their lives are over if they don't make the team. At the U.S. Olympic Trials, just the two fastest on that day make it, so everyone else is unhappy. It's just a tough meet to go through.

A lot of things changed for me after not making the 1996 U.S. Olympic team. I took three months off, which was refreshing. I had taken time off here and there, but never a long period. I also took my first job ever coaching a summer club in Berkeley. I did a lot of thinking about my swimming and decided to take a risk and switch coaches. I started working with the assistant coach at Cal at the time, Eran Goral. He coached the distance swimmers.

All of those events—not making the U.S. team, getting a job, taking time off, switching coaches—took me to a new level. When I started training with Eran I was out of shape from my time off. In high school and at Cal the training was intense, but it was nothing compared to this.

Eran had me do distance work, something I had never done before. He expected a lot from his swimmers in terms of doing things right. He was very good with discipline, but in a way I had not experienced before. Under him I had discipline in school, out of the pool, and in the pool. I owe everything to him. I'd never be where I am now without him.

We had to be on time for practice. We swam two hours in the morning and two hours at night, whereas before I had done dry-land training for part of the workout. I'm the type of person who, when the coach challenges me, I love to accept the challenge. He expected so much mentally and physically. I became the leader of the group. I was in awesome shape. I was getting the best times in the pool, and in the classroom I was getting the best grades of my life. His philosophy was straightforward: focus on one workout at a time, every day. Don't worry about the meets and the results—focus on the process. He said that if I concentrated on every individual workout and did as many things correctly as possible, I could build on it.

After several months, I felt like I had accomplished some great things. It gave me the confidence I needed. Eran taught me to gain confidence for competition through the workouts and training. And that worked. I came to the pool and trained and practiced. He gave me sets to do and I did them. I couldn't believe the times I was doing on workouts.

I look back on the swimmer I used to be, and I'm not even the same. I'm so much better. I could kick the "old me" around now. I didn't know how to get things done before. I was clueless.

Everyone goes through a process of maturing. Things happen for a reason. Eran really helped me out. With two months of school left in 1997, I was getting ready for the world championships in

April. But Eran was leaving the team to go home to coach in Israel. I had to make a decision. My first thought was that I wanted to train with the fastest freestylers, Chad Carvin and Ryk Neethling, who were at the University of Arizona.

But I had to get there first. I called the Arizona coach, Frank Busch. Ironically, he was coming to San Francisco with his son to visit a private law school his son was to attend. Frank and I met for two hours. Because of Eran, I was a very changed person and swimmer. I told Frank what I had been doing and he told me what he could offer me. We agreed and that was it.

When I first came to Arizona, those guys were kicking my behind. But, just like before, I was patient, as a swimmer has to be. After a month, my times were closer to theirs. After a couple of months, I was occasionally beating them. It was so great training with them.

I've been working hard with a goal of making the 2000 U.S. Olympic team.

Though I was not born here, I am a very proud American. I believe in what America stands for. When I think about America I think of it as a country that wants to do things the best, but do them right, honestly, and fairly. We have good leadership in this country.

I love the people in our program. The director of U.S. swimming, Dennis Pursley, wants us to have pride. When we travel abroad, Dennis wants us to win medals, but more importantly, he expects us to represent the U.S. with dignity. I don't think other countries' teams have the privilege we have, of being taken care of and having our needs met by our sport's governing body.

I love hearing the national anthem at our meets; I get chills every time. I love it.

SARAH LEITH
CANOE/KAYAK

Name: Sarah Leith
Sport: Canoe/Kayak
Born: January 10, 1977, Detroit, Michigan
Family: Parents, Toby and Marty Leith; Brother, Corby Leith
Resides: Bethesda, Maryland
Trains: Bethesda Center of Excellence
Coach: Silvan Poberaj

Accomplishments: Member of the U.S. junior team in '93, '94, '95; placed 10th in '94 junior worlds; placed second in the '95 junior pre-worlds; member of the '96 national U.S. team 6th boat; again U.S. team member in '98–6th boat; third place at '98 national championships; U.S. national team member in '99—2nd boat. (To be named to the U.S. national team an athlete must be in the top six at team trials, to actually get to race in the World Cups and world championships must be in top four at U.S. team trials)

Hobbies: Skiing, ice hockey, tennis, sailing, water skiing. But most importantly, when I am not kayaking I try to spend time with my family.

Post-Olympic goals and plans: Graduate from college, then perhaps business school or law school. There is a small part of me that would like to be a teacher.

By Sarah Leith

My Olympic experience not only encompasses the sport of kayaking, but extends to the classrooms of my schools as well.

My grade school experiences were horrible. My brother and I

had learning disabilities, but the teachers thought we were just lazy. They didn't think we were troublemakers or anything—indeed, they knew we were good kids—they just thought we didn't try at school.

The whole experience was traumatic. I remember in fourth grade my teacher asked me to read aloud and I looked down and said, "I can't read it." She yelled, "You haven't tried. You haven't done your homework." I tried to hide the tears, but the pain ripped so deeply into me that I often cried. I really did try. I just didn't know how to read.

We started school in Grosse Pointe, Michigan. The school didn't have a program to detect or deal with learning disabilities. We were helped on tests or papers, but none of the help would have a long-term effect. It was enough to get us through a project or grade and send us on our way.

I remember one teacher who had frizzy red hair and long purple fingernails. When we had tests she said, "When any of you finish the test, you can come up and get a candy sucker." I always finished last. So when I went to get a sucker, all the goods ones (cherry and orange) were gone. I'd get stuck with the ones no one else wanted (lime or lemon).

We also had spelling charts on the board each week. If a student got a 100 on a spelling test he got a star next to his name. So all of our names were on the board, and some kids had at least four or five stars next to their names. I never had a star next to mine.

We moved to Boston, Massachusetts, as I entered fifth grade. One of my teachers said, "You can't read or spell. We have to get you tested." I tested at second-grade reading and spelling levels. The teachers asked, "How did you get through this all the way to fifth grade?"

I felt so stupid.

I wasn't able to do regular classes. I was with a tutor the whole time and was diagnosed with dyslexia. My school didn't have a program to deal with it, but they referred my parents to several schools that could.

The two schools that could help me were at least an hour's drive away. But if I had to attend those schools, I wouldn't be able to participate in sports. Sports were important to me because I could succeed there and feel good about myself.

My parents understood my feelings and enrolled me in a public school. I had a tutor in the afternoon and went to a special class for English. I remember the first book in that class had a number "2" on it—meaning for second-graders. But with the help of my tutor, I was able to work my way all the way up to the book with a "6" on it—my grade. I was very proud.

Things started getting better from then on out. In seventh grade I still had the tutor and special classes. I started feeling better about myself because I was able to read and spell. I had more self-esteem. That was the best part. My tutor told me, "You can overcome these things. You learn just fine. It's just that you learn differently."

In eighth grade, we moved back to Grosse Pointe and I returned to the same school that had not diagnosed my learning disability. At that point I didn't believe I could get As. I thought students with learning disabilities could be satisfied with Cs. I didn't know any better.

For high school I went to Proctor Academy in Andover, New Hampshire, a boarding school that specializes in learning disabilities. They have a great program and it is where I completed the 180-degree turn. I discovered that I could get As and Bs. I finally felt normal. That school used a method that allowed me to learn, so it was a match in academia heaven. I felt that I could be the number one person in my class. I didn't settle for Cs or Bs. Instead, I focused on working as hard as I could for an A in each class. Graduating tenth in my class was another huge boost in self-confidence.

I've gone to a couple of colleges and amassed a 3.75 grade point average. Getting a B now is difficult for me to accept. The experience at Proctor showed me I wasn't any different from anyone else except that it took me two hours to complete a task a mainstream student could do in ten minutes. I had the time, and I worked to close that gap.

I wouldn't trade my learning disability for anything. The dyslexia has made me who I am. It taught me about myself and taught me how to work hard. Everyone has a disability of one form or another to overcome. I'm extremely proud that I was able to overcome mine. No matter what happens to me in life, this will always be my biggest accomplishment. And I still have to work at it daily.

I can relate to anyone who struggles. And those people relate well to me, too. I just have so much admiration for them. One of my idols will always be U.S. Olympic diver Greg Louganis. Reading about him and watching him on TV inspired me to develop and pursue my own Olympic dream. When I entered fifth grade, I was watched the Olympics on television.

Louganis lit up the sky with his daredevil dives and won two Olympic gold medals. My mother said, "Greg Louganis is just like you—he is dyslexic." At that time, there was a flicker of hope in me, a spark I hadn't felt before. Before hearing about Greg, I never realized that anyone with dyslexia could amount to anything. He overcame dyslexia, and he's such a good person. I have never met him, but I feel like I already know him.

As for role models, I look to my parents. I don't like it when athletes are portrayed as role models for making it to the podium or to professional sports. That doesn't necessarily speak to the character they have or what kind of person they are.

That being said, I take any role model status I have or may achieve very seriously. I want to show the younger kids that they are capable of overcoming challenges. I've always felt like I've had something to prove. I was either showing I was good enough for school or good enough for sports. But it was more that I had to prove it to myself than to other people. I felt stupid all the time while growing up—and "stupid" is one of those words that cuts to the bone. I never thought I'd be good in school. Now when I go into class, I take it as seriously as I take a race. Before the start, I think, "This race will get everything I have." When I go into a school classroom I think, "I won't leave this classroom until I've done my best."

I got into kayaking because I was a complete tomboy while growing up. I worshiped my older brother, Corby, who was on the

Proctor Academy kayak team. So, of course, I wanted to be on it, too. He went to Adventure Camp when he was 16 to practice, but he didn't want to go alone, so I got to go along. When I discovered Proctor had a team, I was elated. I then learned kayaking was an Olympic sport. "This is great!" I thought to myself. "I can now be like Greg Louganis!" I joined the team.

Sports always kept me going. I could go outside and my hard work always paid off. In school, the hard work never seemed to get results. Eventually, though, all of my hard work did pay off. I overcame my disability. Each time I got knocked down, I got up again. It pains me to see extremely talented athletes who have bad work ethics. Everything in sports and school has come easily to them, which has let them avoid challenging themselves. We have to be challenged to reach our potential.

For as much as I talk about sports, the funny thing is that I'm not really that talented. Any and all success in sports has come from hard work and that carried over into the classroom. Those two things fed each other and fueled my desire to succeed.

I still face the standard adversity that any athlete deals with. The worst one was a shoulder injury in 1994. I felt a pain in my shoulder while I was working out in the kayak. Then in July 1996, I was selected to do the demonstration runs for the Olympic Games in Atlanta. During one of those runs, I badly tweaked my shoulder.

From July until April 1997, I basically couldn't paddle. The X-rays showed nothing so I kept trying to work through it. The shoulder pain worsened, so I took time off. I thought, "I'm not sure I'm ever going to make it back. Everyone is getting better and better. I'm not doing anything. If I do recover, I will be so far behind, what will that be worth?" I was getting beaten badly by girls who never beat me before. I thought, "I should quit. I am miserable and in pain."

In April I was going to try out for the U.S. national team. The pain was so bad I couldn't even make it down the course. Off the water, I couldn't even throw a Frisbee. Running was painful also because the pounding would jostle my shoulder. This was affecting all aspects of my life. I wanted my life back at that point.

An MRI showed at least a loose ligament. I have loose joints to begin with, so we thought that this might be the case with my shoulder as well. I didn't know if I should have surgery. Another kayaker, Dana Chladek, who won the bronze in the 1992 Olympics and the silver in the 1996 Games, advised me to have the surgery. She had gone through a similar shoulder injury and postponing surgery to try the rehab just made it worse. Dana was such a source of inspiration and guidance. We weren't sure the surgery would work and there was a chance the ligament would just loosen again. At that point though, I had nothing to lose. I was almost ready to give up kayaking because of the pain and mental anguish.

So I had the surgery in April 1997. I went under the anesthetic thinking they would just tighten the ligaments. They scoped it and found a complete tear in the ligament.

It sounds odd, but I was so glad they found a tear. Then I knew it wasn't something I could have rehabbed through physical therapy. They put in a tack to fix the ligament. I took almost the whole year to recover.

It was a struggle. But the time away from the sport made me realize how much I truly love paddling. I had to sit on a stationary bike for that year—that was my workout, basically. I figured out that paddling is what I do. I love the training part of it.

After I came to those realizations, I knew that I could come back. But it did take a lot longer than I thought. A lot of the rehab was as much mental as physical. I had to work to rebuild my self-esteem, and I had to get the confidence back that I could push my shoulder and it would hold up.

In the spring of 1998, I went to the U.S. team trials. The top four make it. I ended up sixth. I wasn't really happy. I was glad to make the recovery complete and compete again, but not making the team was a disappointment.

But I think of what Colorado Senator Ben Nighthorse Campbell once said. "There is but one secret to success—don't give up!"

ANGEL PEREZ
CANOE/KAYAK

Name: Angel Perez
Sport: Canoe/Kayak (K-2 500m, K-4 1000m)
Born: Feb. 2, 1971, Havana, Cuba
Family: Wife, Mari; Son, Andres
Resides: Miami, Florida
Hometown: Miami, Florida
Trains: Miami, Florida, San Diego, California
Coach: Jerzy Dziadkowiec

Accomplishments: sixth place—K-4 1,000m at the 1999 Sprint World Championships in Milan, Italy—qualified for the Olympic Games; fourth place—K-4 200m (non-Olympic event) 1999 Sprint World Championships, Milan, Italy; first place—K-4 100m and K-2 200m, 1999 national championships in Lake Placid, New York; second place—K-4 200m and K-2 500m, World Cup No. 3 in Poznan, Poland; earned two fourth place finishes, a fifth and an eighth at the 1998 Sprint World Championships; holds numerous U.S. national champion titles since immigrating to the U.S. in 1993; 1992 Olympian for Cuba; won six gold medals in 1993, five gold medals in 1992, and six gold medals in 1992 at the Olympic Festival (all for Cuba)

Hobbies: Woodworking, reading

Post-Olympic goals and plans: Retire and continue as Junior Olympic coach and as a personal trainer

By Angel Perez

I have always liked the freedom in America. I like to make my own decisions, but in Cuba someone makes decisions for you.

In 1992 at the Olympics, I reached the semifinals. The day before the race I broke a paddle and the Cuban team didn't have the money to replace it exactly. I had to use a different kind, and it didn't go well.

In 1993 I was ready to defect to America. First of all, I looked at the future. The picture I saw wasn't good. I didn't have any real future in Cuba after I retired from my sport. I was already 22 years old, so I knew the future was rapidly approaching.

Two friends and I were going to defect to the U.S. at a meet in Puerto Rico. We quietly made all the plans. But right before the meet, our coach told us Puerto Rico didn't have a course for our sport. The next scheduled trip was to Mexico for high-altitude training, which is something the Cuban team does every year. I thought, "I have to defect now, or never."

We were very secretive in our planning. We were in Mexico for a week competing in the Olympic Festival where I got four gold medals. That next Friday night, May 22, I didn't sleep at all. We caught a bus Saturday afternoon and went to Nuevo Laredo on the Texas border. We asked our taxi driver, "How do we get to America? Who can set us up?" He took us to a park Sunday morning and we met a Mexican man. It was funny, because helping people get across the Rio Grande River to America was big business down there. We had all kinds of guys bartering with us, trying to get us to use them for our defection.

Sunday morning we were very scared. We negotiated for a $300 rate to get across to America. We paid $150 up front, and then we would pay $150 more when we got to America.

We stripped down to our underwear, putting our clothes on a raft that would be pushed across. All of a sudden there were these huge currents. We had about 50 meters to swim in very rough water. The river was so strong that it started taking our raft that had our clothes. We had to go downriver and help the guy get the raft under control.

Because one of the guys I was with had family in America, there was a car waiting for us when we reached the other side. Without even saying hello or talking to each other, we jumped into the vehicle. The border guards stopped us and asked, "Is everyone in here an American?" Our driver said, "Yes, all are." It was incredible.

That night, heading out of Laredo and across Texas, the world stopped for me. We drove past a car dealership that had the biggest flag I had ever seen. The wind was blowing and the American flag was waving majestically. I had goose bumps and a feeling inside me that is hard to put into words. I said to myself, "Wow, I can't believe it. I am here." That flag made a huge impression on me. Finally, the best freedom and opportunity in the world was right in front of me, blowing across the Texas sky for all to see and admire. The Stars and Stripes represent that American dream.

Finally we were able to relax and we drove all night and the next day to Miami. I had a friend who lived there, so I had a place to stay. If the Mexico thing hadn't worked out, I would have still found a way to get to America. I would have done whatever it took to get here.

Back in Cuba they took down all my pictures and medals at the training center. There was a big picture of me from the 1991 Pan Am Games that was thrown in the trash. Two teammates of mine, who defected a year later, said that when the team returned to Cuba a meeting was called. Some representatives of the Communist Party called me a traitor and told the team that when they saw me at an international competition to spit in my face.

At that time I had no U.S. papers. I took a job in Miami at a burglar alarm company where I worked for a couple of years. I always wanted to keep training and paddling. I wanted to represent America and live the American dream.

When I first came to America it was difficult because I had to start at ground zero. The communication barrier was substantial but not insurmountable. A lot of people in Miami speak Spanish, so that helped. My friends there said, "OK you are here, now you have to get a job and work." I thought, "That's exactly what I want to do. I didn't come here to slug around. I want to move forward." I wanted to reach my potential and get better. At first I had to learn the rules and laws of this country, and then how to fit in. Since I didn't have family or any kind of preparation of what to expect, I learned things on the fly.

I never stopped paddling and coaching, however. I started training seriously again in September 1996. Jerzy Dziadkowiec, my coach, approached me at a coach's conference and asked if I wanted to compete and represent the United States. I finally made the U.S. canoe/kayak national team in 1997 after I got the paperwork done, and I was eligible for U.S. citizenship before the 2000 Olympic Games.

Being a part of the U.S. canoe/kayak family is a great experience. I am from another country and yet I am treated so well. I have always felt like maybe I was taking the spot of an American-born athlete, and that is probably the case. But my teammates, coaches, and the U.S. canoe/kayak organization have never made me feel like anything but a part of their family. That's also made me feel like I'm more a part of this great country. I feel like an American through and through, even though I just defected to America in 1993. So if I have a chance to represent this country, I promise I will do it proudly and with dignity. I would like to give back to the sport after the 2000 Games. I want to work in the U.S. canoe/kayak developmental camps for juniors. I want to help the young people and show them what I have learned.

It would mean so much to me to be in the Olympics as a U.S. athlete. If that happens I will do my best for this country for all that it has given me. To me, I am living the American dream, with a wife, a young child, a house, and a great job. America has given me all of this. I want to pay this country back.

In November 1997 I got a job through the USOC Job Opportunity Program at The Home Depot. I love my job. I love to help customers find what they need and I like to work hard. I don't like to sit at my job and look around; I'm happy when I feel useful. My other job, as a coach, is very rewarding. Since 1995, I have been coaching a group of young athletes. Five of them made the 1999 junior national team. Three of them competed at the junior world championship.

The thing I most like about this country is the freedom to do whatever I want. As I grew up in Cuba and learned about the freedoms in America, I thought, "That is the country for me." The United States is a country for all kinds of different people. If you want to act like trash, you will be trash. But if you want to be good at something, you can be if you work hard. Anything is possible if you apply yourself. That's what drew me to America, the endless possibilities. The future is what you make it to be. It can be bright if you work hard, or it can be bleak if you are lazy. The important thing to realize is that it is all up to you, and no one else. You have the freedom to succeed or fail.

In June 1999 I passed the U.S. citizenship test, so all I had to do was wait for the swearing-in ceremony. I still follow what's going on in Cuba.

The media doesn't give Americans the right picture of Cuba. The journalists who go there stay at the nicest hotels and get the best food, so they think Cuba is doing well. But the government controls that environment. I was at a bookstore and saw a book about Cuba with lots of pictures and accompanying text. It described a country that was nothing like Cuba, yet it was a book on Cuba. The best way for journalists to see the real Cuba is to live there for a year or two in a regular neighborhood. Then, when they come back and write about it, they will paint a different picture from what you see on TV and in the papers.

Even though there are negatives, I try to focus on the positive part of Cuba when I talk to people. The communist countries have good sports programs for kids who show an aptitude. (However, I think that this is mostly political propaganda for the world to see and to indoctrinate Cuban youth.). But there is a lot that is negative, and to tell the whole story I can't ignore those things.

The thing I miss the most about Cuba is my family. I haven't seen them in six years, although I do talk to my mom each month. She always asks when I'll come home and see them. I'm like, "Mom, I don't really think I can go to Cuba." As a defector of a Cuban national team, I don't feel my family or I would be safe.

In Cuba, I grew up in a neighborhood where everyone has lived their whole lives. I want to see how my friends are doing. It's very disappointing to see them living at or under the poverty level, but it is too risky for me to visit. And in the communist atmosphere, my mother can't get a visa.

When I first came to America, I could never have thought things would work out like this. I just closed my eyes from day one and moved forward. I always look toward the future. I don't worry about the past, because there is nothing I can do about it. Certainly I can learn from the past and that is important, but I can't change the past, so I must constantly be aware that I need to push forward. I'm a very positive person, and that helped me when I first got here. I always thought to myself, "I am on the right track, I can't get discouraged. Everything will be fine."

It's tough in Cuba right now, because the economy is pretty bad. My family doesn't get a lot of food, and there is no meat. If you want meat, you have to buy it on the black market. But that costs money, and because of the economy, there's not much money. I send my family money each month and it helps a little bit. My family shares everything—my mom goes to get food and then cooks for the whole family. I'm glad I can help a little bit because my family did so much for me.

I have to credit my wife, Mari, for much of my success and for all the support she has given me, especially considering how hard it has been on us with all my traveling. However, I have truly enjoyed all the times my wife and my son have been able to travel, to see me compete, and share the successes. We have a wonderful son, Andres, who was born in 1996. I am looking forward to my son cheering me in Sydney in 2000. We are truly living the American dream. I can think of nowhere else on earth I'd rather be. And that is because the United States is like no other place on earth.

LESLIE MILNE
FIELD HOCKEY

Name: Leslie Milne
Sport: Field Hockey
Born: Oct. 17, 1956, Framingham, Massachusetts
Family: Parents, Douglas and Bessie Rilla Milne;
Brothers, Douglas and Gordon
Resides: Boston, Massachusetts

Accomplishments: Member of 1980 U.S. Olympic field hockey team (team did not compete because of boycott; member, 1984 bronze medal-winning U.S. Olympic field hockey team

Hobbies: Golf, fishing, basketball, yard work, photography

Post-Olympic goals and plans: Currently emergency room doctor at Massachusetts General Hospital

By Leslie Milne, M.D.

My professional career as an emergency room doctor has somewhat paralleled my experience as a member of the 1984 U.S. Olympic field hockey team.

In 1978, I played field hockey for Williams College, a Division III school in Williamstown, Massachusetts. The summer before my senior year in college, I decided to go to field hockey camp in preparation for my final field hockey season. I went to a U.S. field hockey developmental camp (D camp) not even realizing it was also a selection camp toward the national team. The coaches invited me to attend the next week's "C" camp and 42 days later I was still attending camps, eventually being invited to the national team final trial later that year. That was quite a summer. Amazingly, I made the national team that year, as well as the 1980 Olympic team that, unfortunately, did not compete because of the American boycott of the Olympic Games in Moscow.

My route to the national team was not typical for the times. Most of the top players were from the Philadelphia area, also known as the "hotbed of field hockey." There were a few schools at that time—Westchester, Ursinus, and Penn State—producing most of the elite players. I was in a pre-med program at a small liberal arts college in New England and was not really aware of the hockey world several hours to the south. I give the field hockey association much credit and thanks for creating regional camps such as the one I attended, to identify players from other areas who might have potential but not the same opportunities as Philly players.

The 1980 Olympics were a special time in my sport as it was the first time women's field hockey was included on the Olympic program as a medal sport. While the boycott was personally disappointing, it was even more devastating to the women who had been waiting for their first, and probably only, opportunity to compete in an Olympics. Many of them were in their late 20s and early 30s—late in their prime hockey years or even past them. They had waited a long time for this chance and it was suddenly taken from them. This was true of many athletes in many sports. I was lucky. I was only 22 and would have other chances.

My difficulty was deciding about going to medical school or putting that on hold and training for four more years. The answer was remarkably simple. I could go to medical school anytime, but the Olympics come rarely and we had just learned that even the Olympics are uncertain. Thirteen of us from the 1980 team from the 1980 team, re-dedicated ourselves to the lofty goal of becoming Olympic champions in 1984.

Rather than applying to medical school, I began coaching field hockey, lacrosse, and basketball at Harvard in 1979-81 and then moved on to become assistant athletic director at Wheaton (Massachusetts) College in 1981. These jobs allowed me the opportunity to work, as well as travel and train, with the national team.

My teammate, Chris Larson, was working at Boston University at the time. We got up early, climbed over the chain-link fence at 6:00 a.m., and trained together every day on the practice field. We ran, lifted weights, and played very competitive stick-work games. The rule was that the winner of the game could name the punishment that the loser would have to perform. Chris usually won so I ended up in good shape from all my penalties! I did a lot of fingertip push-ups and one-legged jumping rope in those days.

Early in 1982, we received a letter from the national coach, Vonnie Gros, telling us that if we were interested in participating in the 1984 Olympic Games that we should move to Philadelphia to train full time. We had one month to get there. Thirty of us moved, although no housing or funding was provided. We went because we believed there was value in trying to be the best in the world at something, if only for those few Olympic days in Los Angeles in August 1984. Field hockey is not about money or fame, and for that I am grateful.

I was fortunate to earn a $7,500 per year salary to procure jobs for the other players in the Philadelphia area. We had players working in toll booths on the Pennsylvania Turnpike, working in a local hotel, and being security guards at concerts and football games. While it was nice to have an income, it soon became a bit of a conflict with the other players. Not everyone had a job and others did not like theirs. Practices became stressful for me, as the focus was on the job searches and not the play. Because of this, I left this position and picked up odd jobs where I could find them. My focus was back on the field hockey and I was much happier.

The residency program in Philly involved mostly practice. During that time, we only played about seven to ten international matches a year. That is not much by today's standards, particularly when training full time. Some people were bored by this routine, but I loved it. Having been in a very academic setting all my life, I was like a kid in a candy shop, finally having the chance to explore my athletic side and see how far it could take me. I was lucky because I really enjoyed the process of trying to become great. I think it would have been a very long two years if the only joy one gleaned from this whole experience was playing in the 16 days of the Olympic Games. Every day was fun for me as I had so much to learn to catch up with the players who had been playing internationally for years. The journey itself was most rewarding.

Our coaches, Vonnie Gros and Marge Watson, worked very hard on the psychological part of the sport. They made dealing with adversity a critical part of our training. They worked us hard and when we thought we were done they put us through another harder drill. After an 18-hour plane ride, they had us playing in an international match within hours of landing. We played in the rain, in the snow, and in the heat. Whining was not part of the program.

In 1983, at the Olympic Sports Festival in Colorado Springs, the 1984 Olympic team was named. I think the decision to name the team a full year ahead of the Games was a very insightful one by our coaches. Many coaches wait until the last minute to name their teams, hoping that it will keep the players competitive and avoid complacency. Our coach realized our group was not complacent and that it was more important that we jelled as a team rather than to continue to compete against each another. This was particularly important to me as I always felt I was on the borderline of being selected. Once the team was named, my confidence soared and I worked even harder to prove that my selection was not a mistake.

At the 1984 Olympic Games in Los Angeles, the format for field hockey was round robin, single pool. Although we fared pretty well, we left our last game in fourth place overall, thus believing we were just one spot out of the medals. The point standings were based on win-loss record as well as goals for and goals against. Although a bit confusing, basically our fate depended on the result of the Holland vs. Australia game on the last day of competition. The winner of that game was the gold medalist. Our only chance to medal was if Holland beat Australia by a score of 2-0 or more. If Australia scored even one goal, it put them ahead of us in the "goals for" category, the more important of the tiebreakers. Our chances did not look good.

We watched the game from the stands, quite downtrodden. We

had trained full-time for two years with the expectation of a medal and the hopes for a gold and we were depending upon someone else to get us there. Well into the second half the score remained 0-0. The medal ceremony was to take place immediately after this game. The flag bearers were in the corner of the stadium holding the flags for Holland, Germany, and Australia. Late in the second half, Holland scored a goal to make it 1-0. Our spirits cautiously lifted. The Dutch would easily win the gold with this score.

I will never know if the Dutch team realized our situation, but suddenly their level of play lifted and for the final seven minutes they looked like they were playing for us. Finally they scored the second goal and the game ended 2-0. We had been doing rapid calculations in our heads and realized we were tied with Australia in every category and there would be an immediate stroke-off (shoot-out) between the U.S. and Australia. We rushed onto the field. Our five strokers hurried into uniforms and our goalkeeper padded-up. We had a second life! Our strokers (Sheryl Johnson, Julie Staver, Judy Strong, Beth Anders, Chris Larson-Mason) confidently stepped forward and scored on every attempt and our goalkeeper (Gwen Cheeseman) made phenomenal saves. We had gotten ourselves to the medal stand. It was bronze, but it was beautiful. Australia was devastated, having lost all three medals in one game. To this date, it remains the only U.S. medal in womens' field hockey history.

The flag bearers scurried around to find an American flag and there were plenty around! We all donned our uniforms as the entry march for the ceremony began. It was the Dutch national anthem, but we were singing along. At that point, I am not sure we would have been any happier had it been "The Star-Spangled Banner." We had been lifted from the depths of despair to the highest high of our lives.

It is important to know what you are going to do the day after the Olympics. It can be a tremendous let down once the flame goes out. I spent several mornings at the Olympics studying for my medical school entry tests and made my applications out shortly after returning home. I was accepted at Temple Medical School in

Philadelphia for the class entering in 1985. I was 27, older than most of my classmates, but I considered this to be to my benefit. I had been away from the books for six years, had had my day in the sun and was eager to return. Many of my classmates were coming from competitive pre-med programs and had not had time to experience anything else. Some were bitter and some were burned-out. I felt lucky to be there and was quite enthusiastic about the whole thing. While no one really "likes" medical school, it is an incredibly interesting experience because so much is learned at such a fast pace. My adversity training from field hockey got me through innumerable long nights and exams. I continued to play field hockey on the club level, realizing that balance was important in my life and always feeling free when back at my sport.

Through this time I had the support of my parents and the man who became my husband in 1989, George Nelson. He was the one who always made sure that I did not lose sight of the fact that sport was supposed to be fun. When it is not, we must stop. I have always had fun with sport.

George and I had dated for 15 years and unfortunately, in 1989, he was diagnosed with metastatic cancer. So, after a 15-year courtship, we had a three-week engagement, got married on New Year's Eve of 1989 and headed for San Diego in 1990 for my residency. We had an incredible 16 months together before his death in 1991. I can honestly say that marrying this man was the most important thing I have done in my life. Sometimes we lose sight of what is really important. We get caught up in our jobs or sports careers and become completely self-absorbed. Life events such as this take you back to the basics.

In 1996 I moved back to the East Coast to my current position as an emergency room physician at Massachusetts General Hospital. Like sports, there are rapid decisions made in the emergency room. We try to work as a team to deliver the best care to the patient. Sometimes, even the best decision is not enough to save someone who is critically ill. It is important in both settings that you learn from your experiences and move on. It is easy to get down, particularly if there is a bad outcome. None of us is perfect and we must live with this. Again, it is important to enjoy the journey, as this is where we spend most of our time.

Saving a life or making a difficult diagnosis is very rewarding. Despite television coverage to the contrary, most of what we do in the emergency room is fairly routine. We save lives but we also treat colds, repair sprained ankles, and remove beads from children's noses. I enjoy the variety and the challenge of what might be coming through the doors next. Every day I see something I have never seen before so the learning process is ongoing. The hardest part of my job is telling a family that a loved one has died. It never gets easier, and there is always that heart-wrenching moment when the reality strikes. However, I think having had a loss of my own makes me better prepared to deliver this kind of news.

I continue to play club hockey at a slower, but happy, pace. I am involved with the U.S. elite field hockey teams as chairperson of their High Performance Committee. I guess hockey will always be my passion. My medal is tucked away in a drawer so I can bring it out to show people. They like to touch it and feel like part of the Olympics. It is nice to be able to share it. The reality is that no one wins a medal by himself. We all have coaches, families, and friends who have been there when we needed them. They have taught us skills, cooked us special "welcome home" meals, tried to learn our sport so we would have someone to practice against, and picked us up from the airport after our tours. These people are critical to the experience and should be rewarded, too.

So the journey continues. I would not change a minute of it and eagerly anticipate the next chapter. I am grateful that sport has taken me around the world and back home again. I am happy that I still get goose bumps when I hear our national anthem and see the U.S. flag raised for an Olympic champion. There is nothing else like it, except maybe the Dutch national anthem, just one time, on Aug. 10, 1984.

MICHAEL NORMENT
SWIMMING

Name: Michael Norment
Sport: Swimming
Born: May 13, 1975, New Hyde Park, New York
Family: Parents, Rosemarie and Nathaniel Norment Jr.;
Brother, David Norment; Cousin, Natalie Norment Gladney
Resides: Athens, Georgia
Hometown: Freeport, New York; Philadelphia, Pennsylvania
Trains: University of Georgia
Coach: Jack Baurle

Accomplishments: Swims for Philadelphia Parks and Recreation Department; 1997, 1999 U.S. Pan Pacific team member; 1999 spring U.S. nationals, fifth place in 100-meter breaststroke; 1998 summer nationals, second (100m breast) and fourth (200m breast); 1998 NCAA Championships, seventh (100m breast) and eighth (200m breast); 1997 Pan Pacifics, consolation champion (100m breast).

Hobbies: Drawing, cycling, music, cooking, history, reading

Post-Olympic goals and plans: Continue swimming, pursue coaching career, put college degree (education major) to use by teaching high school history and political science

By Michael Norment

My mother enrolled me in a learn-to-swim program in New York when I was five years old.

That was my start in the sport, and it was fun. My parents wanted me to swim because they didn't want me to play any of the big contact sports because of the injury factor.

I hated swimming the first two or three years. The friends I made at the pool were what kept me in the sport. I was a skinny kid who didn't like the cold water. I also didn't like getting up at 6 a.m., plus all my other friends were playing baseball or football. So it's a good thing that I had made such good friends in swimming.

My parents are probably the reason I'm still in the sport and stayed with it through the years. My parents, and how they handled everything, were a blessing. They didn't know a lot about swimming and they weren't overbearing, as many parents in any sport can be. My father, a standout football player and track star during his high school years, knows a little about swimming, but I like the way it is because no matter how I do, my parents are behind me 100 percent. They always tell me I've done a good job because I did my best. To me, that is the ideal situation for any athlete.

When I was 12 years old, I went to what was called a "Zone All-Star" meet in Buffalo, New York. The Zone All-Star was one of the first turning points in my swimming career because it gave me a totally different outlook on swimming. My perception of fast swimming completely changed. While I was at the meet I caught the attention of a coach from Philadelphia named Jim Ellis. I had read an article about him and the PDR swimming team and had been interested in training with them. I also had come to a point where I had to decide if I wanted to take swimming seriously. My father also had been at the meet and had heard of the PDR swim team. He was aware of Jim's accomplishments and wanted me to have the opportunity to get some real training, knowledge and experience that would eventually help me in my swimming career.

The point that I want to make is that there were plenty of places in New York to train, but I did not feel comfortable training with a white team at the time. My feeling had nothing to do with skin color. Instead, it had more to do with the mindset of white coaches and their philosophies on coaching black swimmers. I had not seen any strong relationships between black swimmers and their white coaches. Also, it was my perception that many of these coaches were dead set on turning all of their black swimmers into sprinters.

Most of the swimmers only swam the 100- and the 50-meter freestyle. Jim Ellis was the first coach I knew who had a great relationship with his swimmers. My first conversation with him gave me the impression that he was a swimming guru, which he is. Jim expanded my horizons in the world of swimming. I love him as a coach and a person; he is like a second father to me. Without Jim's tutelage, I would not have made it to where I am today. He was proud of me for doing well.

"I think you can make the Olympics," Jim told me.

I decided to dedicate more time to swimming. I went to the junior nationals in 1990 as a nervous 14-year-old. It didn't go well at all. I had been the fastest at home, but at nationals the competition was really good all the way across the board, which was a first for me. It took five junior nationals before I performed at a competitive level.

For example, when I was 15 I was seeded first in the 200 -meter breaststroke at junior nationals and I got close to last place. I had to mature quite a bit.

A lot of it was getting used to competing at that level. Once I did that I was fine. All through high school I had no major breakthroughs.

I went to college at the University of Georgia and it was there where I made my breakthrough. It was my first time of going to big meets and consistently placing high.

I went to the U.S. Olympic Trials in 1996. It's a totally different meet. The key is to be normal and relaxed, but focused, because 95 percent of the people there are scared. I took 14th place, which was tough. I had dreamed about being there for such a long time, yet it was the biggest nightmare. There were people there I knew I could beat, but didn't.

I wondered what went wrong. I struggled that year with training leading up to the trials, and even got sick from over-training. But I thank God for that year; had I not gone through it I would not have figured out what I needed to do.

I was really down after I swam. My parents and brother asked me if I was all right when we were back at the hotel because I was sulking. My brother asked, "Will you keep training for 2000?" I looked up and said, "Yes." Everyone started cheering and hugging me. "Don't worry about money or anything else, we'll be there for you."

That instilled a fire to keep training. I approached my coaches with my thoughts on what I needed to change. My coaches started to see me as a man instead of a student-athlete, and that took our relationship to a different level.

I reached a new level of confidence and maturity and really started improving. I came home to Philadelphia and saw my brother working two or three jobs but keeping a 3.8 grade point average in school. My father was traveling, teaching five classes and writing books. I had friends from high school who had to quit college at various points to work full time and save money. All I had thought about my freshman and sophomore years of college was swimming. I looked at my situation and decided I was sitting on a free education and throwing it away.

So in the summer of 1996 I decided to have a life outside of swimming, because if I thought only about swimming all the time it would drive me crazy.

I went to my coach at Georgia, Jack Baurle, and said, "Jack, I need to sprint." My training had to change a little bit. I saw opportunities where before I had seen obligations.

To that point I was not competing up to my potential. In 1997, I used the motivation of not making the Olympic team in 1996 to push me. I shaved 1.5 seconds off my time in the 100-meter breaststroke in 1997, which is a huge amount of time. So I'm on track for my goals, but I have a lot of hard work in front of me.

A lot is made of the fact that I am a black swimmer. In some ways, if I look at it that way it can limit me. Different ideas break into a person's head.

Without regard to race, I want to be the fastest swimmer in the 100-meter breaststroke, not just the fastest black swimmer in that event. I would greatly enjoy the notoriety of being the first African-

American to make the Olympic swim team. My first goal is to win, but if I think about being the first black swimmer, it moves the focus away from my goal.

Swimming has been a predominantly white sport. But I'm a swimmer. I don't think of it in terms of skin color. If I work and achieve my goals, the other things will follow.

We had a predominantly black team in Philadelphia under Jim, but we wanted people to see us as a fast team, not a fast black team. We wanted to show the world that we were swimmers and talented kids. You do see more black faces now and that is great.

Seeing a black swimmer who is doing well can inspire young black kids to get into the sport. It's a great feeling to know that Byron Davis and I, along with other black swimmers, have made them feel like they can do it, too. The worse thing any child can think is that he can't do something because of race, whether it's black, white, Hispanic or whatever.

There's a lot of negative mythology in the sport of swimming. I met someone in Georgia who said, "Wow, you're a swimmer, I didn't know black people could swim." To be honest, there is still a stigma with black people and swimming.

I don't mind being viewed as a role model. But it all has to do with being a good person. I'm flattered when I am called for an interview. Plus, I never know where I am going to be years down the road. I will run into the same people again and I have to give back.

I was helped by one of my friends, Stan Beechman, a sports psychologist. He asked me during my freshman year, "How many guys at the NCAA Championships think they can win it?" I thought perhaps 10. But the difference, Stan taught me, between winning and eighth place isn't really talent or ability. It's learning how to be a great swimmer. I knew I had the ability when I was a freshman. I had to learn what I needed to fix to be better.

In those four years at Georgia I learned what it took to perform at the highest level. It was just a matter of putting the right things together.

The hardest struggle in college is to go a couple of years and not improve. In college I didn't improve a whole lot, maybe a second or so in the 100 and two seconds or a little more in the 200. It's tough to train for years and not drop any real time. But that's where the sport of swimming is unique. All of a sudden, after three years of not improving, there can be a breakthrough as I had in 1997.

With all the training in this sport, a person has to love it to stay with it. Most swimmers who join the sport don't think about getting paid or making a living from it. The focus is on swimming fast.

What a swimmer invests in the sport dictates how long he wants to stay in the sport. Having the desire to succeed and swim faster to gets him through the day-to-day workouts. In late winter, a swimmer doesn't want to be in the pool. But keeping the perspective that time will pass and the work will pay off helps. Learn to deal with things and don't look at bad experiences as negatives. View them as learning experiences.

I'm always striving to get better. That carries itself out of the water to how I study and how I can become a better person. Swimming gives a work ethic that will help in life. That's why it's such a good sport for kids, because that discipline and dedication is something that isn't being instilled in kids today like it was in the past.

Becoming a better swimmer takes time. A lot of kids, especially teens, want that immediate gratification of seeing great results right away. But in any profession, it won't work that way. Work hard to make things fall into place.

Compared to other things in life, swimming is hard. I put a lot into it. But I learn how to deal with people, tension, adversity and other difficulties that I will face in different areas of life. I think about the commitment swimming requires, and I have to believe it will help me when I get out of the pool for the final time.

MARY LOU RETTON
GYMNASTICS

Name: Mary Lou Retton
Sport: Gymnastics
Born: Jan. 24, 1968, Fairmont, West Virginia
Family: Husband, Shannon; Daughters, Shayla and McKenna
Hometown: Houston, Texas
Coach: Bela Karolyi

Accomplishments: Five medals, gold, two silvers, two bronze (won the all-around gold) in the 1984 Olympics; won three straight America's Cups (1983-1985)

Hobbies: Cooking, reading and exercising

Post-Olympic goals and plans: Being a mom, continuing speaking career

By Mary Lou Retton

I always had fun doing gymnastics. I stayed in the sport for so long and excelled in it because I loved it. I am a passionate, emotional woman who wears her heart on her sleeve. So when I am having a good time, I show it. I'm glad that it also has given others happiness.

People ask me where my love for gymnastics, and my competitiveness, was born. I'm the youngest of five children and we grew up in a competitive, positive environment. My parents introduced us to an array of sports and interests. They wanted us to find things we enjoyed and they always encouraged, but not pushed, us to have a good time and take pride in whatever we pursued.

I loved cheerleading, track and field, swimming, and dance. I also loved gymnastics. Around age 11, I decided to focus on gymnastics. It was the sport where I excelled the most. More than anything, my mother was happy when I chose gymnastics because she no longer had to drive me to five other club activities or sports practices!

Selecting gymnastics was solely my choice. I loved it from the first time I walked into the gym.

The road to the 1984 Olympic Games in Los Angeles was a long one. The gymnastics community knew me, but the country and the world did not. Even some of the international judges at the Olympics didn't know me because I had broken my wrist and missed the world championships in 1983.

The sporting world was a different place then, especially at the Olympic level. It truly was the last generation of amateur athletes. Now athletes have agents before they reach the Olympics, and that's fine. But if someone had asked me before the 1984 Games if I had an agent, I would have thought, "Like a travel agent?"

So the 1984 Olympic Games represented my first major international competition. My dream was to wear the red, white, and blue.

I am so patriotic. We were wearing the American flag on our leotards. When we saw them we almost all started crying, we didn't embrace the style right away. But it turned out to be the perfect leotard. America was hungry for a patriotic winner, and those uniforms exuded patriotism. I was lucky that I was involved in one of the glamour sports. Gymnastics doesn't get a lot of coverage in the years leading up to the Olympics, except for some television from nationals and worlds here and there. But in the Olympics, gymnastics really gets a lot of attention. I had nothing to do, of course, with that factor, but it certainly helped with how things turned out for me.

I won the gold medal for the all-around on a Friday night. One of the headlines the next morning was that I had stormed the scene "overnight."

Overnight? No way. It was a long process that took a lot of years and I was happy that things worked out so well. The Lord had a plan for me and that was in the outline.

I was not well known, so there weren't high expectations of me, but there was pressure being in the Olympics. I was able to chase, and attain, my dream. The actual winning of the medals was over in a short period of time, but my life literally changed overnight.

The morning after the gold, Saturday, I was in the Olympic Village with a teammate. We walked outside of the security surrounding the village to order a ring that featured the Olympic rings. The rings were supposed to be ready that day, so I figured I'd just go pick it up. I wasn't aware my life was changing based on winning the night before.

Naïve little me stepped outside the village and I had my first encounter with my so-called "new life." People pulled at me, cameras flashed and people yelled. It was frightening and security pulled me back in.

For as much as my life had changed, I couldn't grasp the meaning of "celebrity." Ironically, I never have grasped or embraced that concept. I am still the same person I always was. My love and dream was gymnastics. It just so happened that most of the world watched me pursue my goal.

But it never changed me. I'm still the same Mary Lou from West Virginia. I was brought up in a Christian home with morals and values and I appreciate my family so much for that. I give my family credit that I was able to keep a level head and be myself. My brothers and sisters would never have let me get a big head. My family is a group of incredible people.

The role model issue is talked about a lot in this day and age. I went to the Olympics to fulfill my dreams, not to become a role model. But that status comes with winning. I remember watching Nadia Comaneci in the Olympics in 1976 when I was seven years old. I remember that feeling of empowerment. I wanted to be just like her, so I looked to her as a role model. So I owed it to the kids who followed me to be their role model, to handle myself well and not set a bad example.

Sure, I've made mistakes, and I continue to make mistakes, but it's really not that difficult to lead a clean life and be the best person you can be. Role models ideally are our parents, siblings, or other people close to us in life. It's just a fact that athletes are looked up to by the nature of exposure through the media. While I encourage children to find role models close to them, I take my role as a role model very seriously and I want to impact children's lives in the most positive way possible.

After the Olympics, I had many endorsement offers that I turned down. I tried to go with legitimate companies that I trusted. I didn't want to sell my name and character, so I decided to go with projects that made sense and promoted a positive message. To be sure, the Olympics rewarded me with plenty of things, but I never let the focus rest on money.

We're more than 15 years removed from the Olympics of 1984. It baffles me that I am still recognized and hear from fans. There are so many multi-gold medalists that I can't fully grasp what caused my run to be etched in the minds of so many. Part of it had to do with the timing. It was 1984 and the Games were here in America. With the political climate and our relationship with the Soviet-bloc, Americans were aching for something to hold onto at that time. Being the first American gymnast to win gold in the all-around made it special, and I am so grateful for that.

Today, athletes are on the cover of magazines and are touted even before the Olympic Trials. So they go to the Olympics and they are expected to win. In my case, the lack of expectations added to the element of surprise. I don't think Hollywood could have written a better script. I had to be perfect on my last event, the vault, to win. Romanian Ecaterina Szabo, who was ahead of me, was already waving to the crowd in anticipation of winning. And then, needing a 9.95 to tie, I hit the vault, scored a 10, and took the all-around gold. I couldn't have set up more drama if I had mapped it out in my own words and thoughts.

Now I am the mother of two wonderful little girls. I have the best job in the world. It's a thousand times more difficult than the Olympics, and a million times more rewarding. Being a parent is the most important job a person can ever have. People ask me, "What do you want to be remembered for?" My goal is to be a gold medal mom. Take my medals, though they were a highlight of my life, but being a mother is a reward that I thank God for every day, and will for the rest of my life.

Everything I learned from the Olympic journey parallels my career as a working mom. It's very difficult to balance being a mother and traveling, so I place limitations on my career. I am never gone for more than one night. My girls know that. They see the suitcase and know that I'm leaving, but they know the rule—I'll be back the next day. If I have to be gone longer, I take them with me.

I want my kids to love what they do in life, just like my parents did for me. When you get to an elite level, no one can force you to work or train. We trained eight hours a day—four in the morning and four at night. No one can force a person to do that. Being forced results in half an effort and half the results. A person has to learn from the journey.

When I was in Houston training for the Olympics I called home crying many times. Physically it was crazy. My body took a long time to adapt to eight hours a day in the gym, especially since I was accustomed to working out two or three hours a day at the most. Going from West Virginia where I was the only elite gymnast to Bela Karolyi's gym where I was maybe the fifth or sixth best took time to adjust to. I wanted to give up so many times. When I called my parents, I said I wanted to come home.

"Sleep on it," my mother and father said. "If you still feel the same way in the morning, call and we'll come get you right away."

After a good night of sleep, I woke up realizing things weren't as dramatic as I thought, so I stuck it out.

There is adversity to deal with in any walk of life. It's difficult for kids to understand that, but failure can be the most motivating tool. We have to learn from failure. We fail at something, work on it more, master that step, and take another.

I work better under pressure. I have the attitude "I'm going to show you!" Bela was a key for me in that regard. Bela was different and tough, but he gets a bad rap because he's not abusive or mean.

Bela knew how to create champions. He wasn't a "yeller." If I missed a vault, he put his head down and then looked at the next gymnast coming down to vault. Boy, that got to me! I wanted that attention. So he motivated me that way because that's what my personality dictated in terms of how to deal with me. Sure enough I'd make the correction and he acknowledged that. Bela did a great job of adapting to the various personalities and temperaments of his students. He is truly a great man, father, and coach.

One of the reasons I'm always upbeat is that I surround myself with positive people. My husband and I are at a stage in our lives where we don't have to do anything we choose not to do. We do things because we want to, with people we like to be around. I use family in a broad term. I include our close friends, as well as our family. Our "family" is filled with positive thinkers who are encouraging. I've seen it happen so many times where there's just one naysayer in a group, one negative force who can bring the whole group down. When that happens, I check out. I am a high energy, positive person, and I don't want to be around people who are negative. That's my choice. And that's why I'm so happy.

People ask, "Are you for real?" I have been told that my smile and constant perkiness get on people's nerves. But that's me. What you see is what you get. I want people to see the positive. I want them to push toward the end of the rainbow, enjoying the journey and reaping the reward that comes from doing a job well done.

If you reach your goal, whether it's making all-state or even just making your high school team, that is a gold medal in life. And everyone has the potential to win that gold and experience that feeling. I am a mother and wife. The fulfillment it brings me cannot be equaled by anything else. The medals are nice and I am so grateful for everyone who made this event so special and meaningful. But it is how you impact people, and how you live your life that really matters.

Offer a smile or encouragement to someone who needs a boost. Not only will you help them, but also help yourself more than you could ever imagine.

SCOTT IKLÉ
SAILING

Name: Scott Iklé
Sport: Sailing
Born: Nov. 23, 1961, Manhasset, New York
Family: Parents, Ulla and Richard; Sister, Lisa; Brother, Keith
Resides: Geneva, New York
Occupation: Head sailing coach, Hobart and William Smith Colleges
Trains: Hobart and William Smith Colleges, New York

Accomplishments: Eight North American or national Championships; 1998 USOC Developmental Coach of the Year-Sailing; 1999 Pan American coach-sailing
Hobbies: Outdoor activities

By Scott Iklé

When I was growing up my parents belonged to a yacht club. I thought sailboat racing would be a great sport to learn. I had always gone to day camps and was never exposed to junior sailing. When I pressed my parents for the opportunity to learn how to race, they said, "Figure it out if you want to do it." So I did.

I was 15 years old and had just gotten my working papers. I knew that I would need to raise enough money to get a boat. I worked that summer as a dishwasher and as a caddy at a local golf course to save up enough money to buy a Laser. By the end of the summer, I had earned about $1,000. The next summer my mother drove me to the Laser dealer. I was scared to part with all the money in my bankbook, but somehow she talked me into buying the boat that day.

I knew the basics of sailing, but when it came to racing I had no idea. That night we took the Laser down to the club for a sail. I was so proud I had a new boat. I rigged up and went out for a sail, only to learn when I got back to the dock that I had rigged the boat wrong. I knew I had a lot to learn. I started to read anything and everything I could on racing tactics and strategy. I would also question any other sailors about the sport whenever I could. I had the opportunity to participate in a couple of local bay races and could finish first or second by the end of the summer in some of the races. I thought this was easy.

So I figured I was ready for the Laser District 8 Championship Regatta by the end of the summer. There were a lot of excellent sailors at that event—college All-Americans, national champions. I finished last in every race, sometimes a whole leg behind. But I wasn't discouraged. Everyone I raced against was incredibly nice. Every time one of the other competitors saw me doing something wrong, they showed me how to do it the right way, and I learned a lot that day. I was having so much fun. I loved being on the water in a fast boat and learning all I could about sailing. Within two summers I was racing every weekend on the district circuit and every once in a while I even won a regatta.

In high school, I was the typical athlete, playing soccer and lacrosse which are big sports here on the East Coast. I decided to attend college at Hobart College (New York) in the fall of 1980. I really had no idea about college sailing. I decided to play lacrosse that year, tried out, and made the team. The following summer I returned home to once again sail in the Laser circuit. I found out that sailors, whom I could once beat, had gotten better by sailing in college. It took the whole summer of training to get back to the point where I could beat them.

When I went back for my sophomore year of college, I realized after playing fall ball that I had gone as far as I could in lacrosse, so I gave it up to sail full time. I knew I was getting better at sailing and decided I would concentrate on it more and see where it took me.

Things just really started to click for me in sailing. I had the opportunity to train and race with and against some great people who were willing to help me and coach me and give advice. I worked hard sailing about six months a year, every day after work or school. I kept reading more and more about the sport and became a student of the game. I worked hard to get good.

That first Laser district championship where I was last in every race became history. By the time I finished college, I had won three district championships and the Empire State Games and qualified to sail in two Laser world championships. I sailed in only one championship, finishing in mid-fleet. I started to sail Grand Prix boats and in the summer of 1984, I won my first national championship in the Olympic class Flying Dutchman.

I raced as much as I could, and one thing led to another. I went from racing on the regional and national circuit to racing on the international scene. When I got out of college, all I did for a number of years was race and work. I have won many regional regattas, taken eight North American or national titles, and finished seven times in the top ten at world championships in a number of different types of boats.

My dream is still to make the U.S. Olympic team, of course. However, now I make my living as a sailing coach, so I also want to help my athletes reach that same goal. I'm in a unique spot where I'm still young enough to be a good international competitor, but if I don't make the Games as an athlete, maybe I can get chosen as a coach.

I actually fell into coaching. After college, I was working for a marina group and racing boats internationally. A friend called up and said the United States Merchant Marine Academy needed a part-time coach. I thought, "Sure, why not?" I started coaching part time as a nice way to supplement my income. The part-time position led to a full-time job as an assistant coach at the Merchant Marine Academy. I found myself leaving my old job so I could coach during the day and attend graduate school at night at Long Island University.

At the same time, the sailing program at my alma mater, Hobart and William Smith was in danger of being cut. At the time, the school had a new president who knew little about the sport. The colleges were looking at programs to cut, and sailing was under a microscope. The students in the sailing program met with the president and the board of trustees to review the needs of the program. I got involved as a consultant to help all the parties. My recommendation to save the program was a coach and 16 boats. I sent in a proposal outlining my ideas.

Since there was no guarantee for the Hobart and William Smith coaching job—or even that there would be a program—I was interviewing for other jobs since my graduate studies were done. I was finalizing a deal for a job when I said, "Excuse me, I have to make a call." I called the president of Hobart and William Smith. I asked him if they were going to save the program and hire me. I told him I had another job literally waiting for me in the next room. I needed a decision. "You have the job for one year, and we will take it from there," Hobart and William Smith president Richard Hersh told me. "But financing the program—you'll have to figure it out." So I became the coach of the program in the fall of 1993.

There were two major challenges in the first year. One, we needed good sailors and two, we needed to fund the program. Recruiting for the program was the first great challenge for the program in its first year. The recruited high school sailors would have to take a big risk. Before they could sail as freshmen, the school, the existing program, and I would have to prove ourselves and make it to the second year. Who knew for sure that we would succeed so they could have their chance?

The first year I actively recruited about 45 people and got seven. At that point, half of our team hadn't even sailed before. All of our early recruits were considered castoffs by other colleges. So my pitch in recruiting was that the student-athlete could go to another college and sit on the bench, or come to Hobart and start. But those so-called castoffs held their own. These were athletes who believed in themselves and were willing to work hard. They also believed in me. In early competitions, we were laughed at all over the place.

Even as the team started to improve and was on the verge of breaking into the national rankings, people said, "It's a fluke. You guys are getting lucky."

Many of our most successful sailors at Hobart and William Smith were recruited by other schools, but would have been part of huge teams and may never have gotten a chance to compete. Two of our sailors came here lightly recruited from other schools. But four years after coming to Hobart, in their senior year they won the 1997 Atlantic Coast Championships overall and in both divisions. They finished third at the national championships after having won both the spring and fall MAISA district dinghy championships, spending most of the year as the number one ranked team in the nation.

But not all of our successful sailors have been recruited. At my first practice as the Hobart and William Smith coach, I walked down to the docks to get everything ready. A young woman, Ady Symonds, came over to me and said, "I've only been sailing a couple of times, but I'd really like to do this. Can I try out for the team?" My response was "yes." Three years later, she walked out an All-American. She had talent. She put in the work. She was a natural athlete, but she had superior drive and a great work ethic.

When the class of 1998 graduated that spring, everyone else thought we'd flounder. We came back in the fall of 1998 and were third in the Atlantic Coast Championships. Even today, we're not one of the most respected programs in the country. People view us as one or two athletes strong. In 1999, I think we really did a good job of putting that myth to rest because we went to four events where we had to sail in multiple divisions—and we won three of the four Regattas. Three of the most important college events of the year. That was a good measure of where we've come from, where we are, and where we're headed. Every year I re-evaluate my goals and try to figure out what the next challenge is going to be.

In the spring of 1999, we went to two national championships, team race (finished third) and women's (finished ninth). The women's team was being laughed at as recently as the spring of 1998. Yet we won the district championship in the spring of 1999, which gave the team a berth at nationals. A lot of our women skippers were recruited by me and maybe a few others. It was the same old story: "If you come here, you won't sail much, but you can be on our team. Maybe you should look somewhere else." But they knew if they chose us, they'd be sailing right away and getting better all the time.

A lot of the sailors we recruited never really made it to a high level as a junior sailor. They came and blossomed. That's the difference between our program and the others: I like to think this program can make you a better sailor, whereas some of the other programs manage you as a sailor. I don't know that a lot of the top junior sailors really improve much at other colleges. That is why we have put 12 sailors on the All-American team, won four district championships in the last four years and gone to five national championships.

But I do know that the sailors who come here, get better. We are among the top five programs in the nation now. We're constantly in the top five rankings and hardly ever have we dropped out of the top ten in the last three years. Yet 30 percent of our team is still at the level where they're really just learning to sail when they get here. We also get a lot of athletes from other sports who for one reason or another decided to stop playing their sport at the college level. Hobart and William Smith has excellent intercollegiate sports, and since some athletes don't meet their expectations in those sports, they come to us.

Our sailing program at Hobart is a structured environment. We lift weights, run, and teach mental training in addition to practicing on the water. The athletes from other sports who join us just love it. Some other sailing coaches talk about training and its importance, but it's not really an integral part of their program. Here, it is mandatory. We don't have a standard that athletes have to meet, but they must improve. As long as students continue to improve in strength and fitness and become better sailors, they will stay on the team. Once the times and test scores drop, and it's obvious the students aren't working, they won't stay on the team.

I have a soft spot for people who are willing to work hard. I like to think I don't have any favorites. But the truth is that anyone who puts in the time and works hard catches my attention. After the success our program at Hobart and William Smith has experienced, I had chances to move on to other programs. I stay here because this is mine. This is my sweat and blood. And this is the school from which I graduated and that I sailed for. I like the athletes I work with. I like the area I live and work in.

It's been incredibly rewarding. I'm not ready to turn around and give someone the keys to the store and say, "Here, it's yours." I know at some point everyone moves on, so it's not realistic to think I will retire here. However, as long as there are still challenges, I will remain. If it comes to a point that I am just maintaining the program at the current level and not making it better, I will leave. I would have to, because I tell my athletes to push themselves and get better—to risk a little more each day. So as a coach, I have to live by the same motto.

IRIS ZIMMERMANN
FENCING

Name: Iris Zimmermann
Sport: Fencing
Born: Jan. 6, 1981, Rochester, New York
Family: Parents, Thomas and Christina Tien Zimmermann; Sister, Felicia
Resides: Rush, New York (Stanford, California, for 10 weeks)
Hometown: Rush, New York
Coach: Buckie Leach

Accomplishments: 1995 and 1997 Cadet world champion; 1997 Junior World Cup champion; 1997 national champion; 1999 World University Games second in team; 1999 Pan-American Games third in team

Hobbies: Talking on the phone, reading the Sunday *New York Times,* squash (a newly acquired hobby)

Post-Olympic goals and plans: Law or business school, open a sports center for inner-city kids with my sister

By Iris Zimmermann

Since my older sister Felicia was involved in fencing, I was taken to the fencing center from the time I was about two years old.

I wasn't very good at swimming or gymnastics, and fencing was just much more interesting and fun to me. I knew a lot of the kids in the sport through Felicia. The fencing center always felt like home. Some things we just get a feeling about, the kind that tells us something is there, and that's how fencing was for me.

When I was younger, I was big for my age, so that physical strength was a plus. I loved going to the fencing center, too. Sure, practice can seem like the same old routine day after day. But if we know what we want to do and know what it takes to improve and are having fun, practices often don't become mundane. There are always challenges each day, and thus the opportunity for more progress.

At the Cadet Worlds in 1995 I was the underdog, and it's so much easier than being the favorite. I had nothing to lose and everything to gain. Winning the Cadet Worlds that year was the best. The greatest challenge, though, lies in the ability to duplicate a winning performance because there is more on the line—everything to lose and seemingly little to gain.

The first win was utter happiness and an overall great time. The second time was proving the first time was not a fluke. The climb to the top is easier than staying on top. Those at the top are hunted, but that can be used as an advantage. People fence me harder and that motivates me to train harder. I use it as a strength because people are scared to fence me. When we are the prey, we fight partially out of fear and we don't always get our opponents' best effort because they are thinking about the top fencer they have to go against. At this point, I know I have the skills to beat those who are "after" me. I used to have a problem with that, but I realized I worked hard and now I have the confidence to approach those scenarios with the right mindset.

Now I know my opponents will give me only their best shot. You know what? That's how I want it. I don't want to get anything less than my opponent's best shot. It's definitely a positive when someone gives me his best because it means I am where he wants to be. So I stay on my toes.

I'm looking for results not just for me, but for the United States, because I want to keep this program headed toward the top level in the world. If it takes results from me, or someone else on our team, I want to do whatever it takes. I love being in this position. We're all paving the road, and I'm hoping the fencers who follow me in the years to come do even better. It's great that we now have the attitude that we can, and should, win. We have to push ahead.

The fencers who really started this march for the U.S. were Ann Marsh and Felicia. They cleared the path with a swath, and it's up to us to pave it and continue the process they started. We want that path to be paved and we want those who come after us to march proudly up that road and achieve even higher goals and set higher standards.

Not being taken seriously as a fencing country always gave me motivation. It drives me to excel. We win and think, "You underestimated us. We're here to medal." It excites me to show everyone our team is a force to be reckoned with.

We have to believe in ourselves, first and foremost. At the World University Games in 1999, I told my teammates, "I don't know what you came here to do, but I came here to win. Let's do it."

At the 1998 Seven Nations competition in February in Germany, I suffered a lateral meniscus injury in my left knee. It's hard to come back from because the meniscus is the padding between the bones and the knee. The injury made me realize how lucky I am to be strong and young.

We get so stuck on the competition that we don't take a step back, sometimes until we are forced, and look at the big picture. It is so important to enjoy the journey. Yes, we have to push ourselves, but when we are done we have to know we had fun and gave it our all. If we don't enjoy ourselves, and if it is not coming from the heart, we won't do well. I have that appreciation, and I know I am very lucky to do this.

It was really difficult for a while. In the beginning, I thought, "I'm injured but I'll come right back." So what happened? I re-injured my knee. I have had two surgeries and came back twice, and the second time was harder. I thought, "Will I re-tear this?" I did everything wrong during the first comeback. I questioned myself a lot, especially when I had to come back a second time. If an athlete does not believe in himself he has defeated himself before he has faced his first opponent.

I think the physical part is easier than the mental part in getting my confidence back. The healing powers the human body possesses are so amazing, which makes the physical comeback much easier than the mental. It is our mind that takes the longest to heal.

I finally figured out during the rehab from the second surgery that, "I will be better than I was before." My motivation was the 2000 Olympics, and my sister, Felicia. She told me, "I've been injured before. You're young and strong. You have so many years ahead of you. Stay patient." One of the other fencers, Cliff Bayer, had the exact same injury and surgery during the Olympic year in 1996. Seeing him come back successfully was inspiring. Cliff and I are close, like brother and sister. Seeing him go through what he did and how he handled it made me realize, "My career is not over. I'm 18 years old and I have nowhere to go but up."

I always had it in the back of my mind to get to the Olympics. I never said, "Yes, I'll train for the Olympics." There are other goals with the world championships and everything, but certainly watching the Olympics on television provided great motivation. I watched it on TV and said, "I know I'm going to be there someday."

The skills I've learned in fencing will help in the real world, just as with all sports. They teach us to deal with adversity and it shows us what it takes to compete. On top of all that, it makes us master time management, which is critical to success in all aspects of life. Athletes who go into business have had to balance school and sports plus work in most cases. That helps in any career, so use those skills to get ahead in the real world.

I'm very patriotic, fiercely so. I love the feeling of representing the United States, the best country in the world. I come back from trips and I want to kiss the ground, and sometimes I do. My parents are immigrants. My father is from Germany and my mother is from China. I realize the reason they came here was opportunity. I have that opportunity because of their courage so I want to seize that.

I love wearing the USA warmup outfits. A lot of people trade warmups with other countries. Not me. I'm not interested in wearing another country's name on my back. I'm proud to have "USA" on my back.

I've also learned from traveling to other countries. It's made me realize how fortunate we are to live in the United States. I realize there are opportunities afforded to Americans and that I should not just be grateful, but I should go out and do the best I can. We have the best situation of anyone. I have access to anything I need or want, from nutritionist to sports psychologists and equipment. All of that motivates me.

This whole experience has shown me that my sister and I can achieve whatever we set our minds to. We set our goals high. It's been so much fun to have Felicia be a part of this and have her be among those paving the way. She casts a big and long shadow. It has made me want to work hard, not just to achieve what she has, but to do more. The support she has given me is amazing.

Sports are huge for young kids. It can give them self-confidence and self-esteem, which is very important in this era. It seems like kids have low self-esteem more than ever. Sports give them the skills they need to develop as people. They have to come home from school and do their homework before they train. They learn to know themselves, what they can accomplish, how their personality fits in with a team and how they can reach goals. More than ever kids need to be a part of a team, and in fencing, it's like a family.

Kids need to know they have people they can trust and turn to when things get tough. I take the status I've earned through fencing very seriously. I know the kids I speak to or interact with are impressionable, and kids need great role models. Being a role model can be scary, though. I constantly keep myself in check because I don't want to do anything that would cast me in a negative light.

We must have people around us who motivate and drive us. We also must have that drive inside ourselves. We need to learn from the teachers and coaches we have. My mother is very philosophical about that. If I'm complaining about a coach or teacher, my mother reminds me, "Teachers are people you respect. They teach you lessons in life that are invaluable and that you will carry the rest of your life."

TONY DEBOOM
TRIATHLON

Name: Tony DeBoom
Sport: Triathlon
Born: Nov. 12, 1968, in Cedar Rapids, Iowa
Family: Mother, Sandi; Brothers, Todd, Tim, Tom; dog, Thor
Resides: Colorado Springs, Colorado
Trains: United States Olympic Training Center,
Colorado Springs, Colorado
Coach: Dr. Peter Gorman

Accomplishments: 1999 Pan Am Games; 1999 Pan Am Trials, first place; 1999 Pucon (Chile) Internationals, fourth place; 1999 U.S. Triathlon Series, Oceanside, sixth place

Hobbies: My dog is my biggest hobby, also movies, sketching, and writing.

Post-Olympic plans: I will focus the remainder of my career on the Hawaiian Ironman. After racing, well, we'll just have to see.

By Tony DeBoom

In 1987, I was accepted to West Point and began my career in the U.S. Army. My younger brother, Tim, followed two years later.

Tim was thinking about leaving almost immediately. My parents and everyone at West Point told him to stick it out, that things would get better. It's not uncommon for first-year students to want to leave—UCLA sounds good to everyone that first year.

I used to sneak him off the post to take him to movies, trying anything I could to help him. But after a year, he still wanted to leave. I realized he was looking for someone to give him that push out the door. I knew he wanted to realize his goals in the triathlon.

Life is short, and a person shouldn't do anything he is unhappy with. So I gave him that final push to leave because I knew that's what he wanted. I respected him for taking that leap—it takes a lot to leave a service academy. A student is pressured to stay, and it's not like transferring at a civilian institution.

When I graduated in 1991, I decided to challenge myself, so I wanted to be an Army Ranger—if I were going to be in the Army, I wanted to be Rambo. To this day, that training—especially the Airborne Ranger School—is the hardest thing I've ever done. It's not so much what we did, but what we did without. We did without sleep, without food. There was a pretty high dropout rate.

Being in the infantry is a rough life: You live, eat, and breathe it. There is very little time to be alone. When I had time I trained for the triathlon or talked on the phone to Tim. I was depressed—I was not happy with my job.

My Army experience helps me in terms of discipline—that is, it never occurs to me to skip training. Going to practice or swimming is my duty. That's a good quality I took from the Army. Some people will say, "Well, I don't feel like training today, so I'll forget it, and do double tomorrow." My brother and I aren't that way. The West Point experience and how we were raised has made it easy for us to ignore those feelings and to do what we need to do.

West Point also gave me a sense of loyalty to people who are loyal to me, like my family, friends, and sponsors. I will always sacrifice for them. My military experience also made me appreciate what this country stands for, and the sacrifice the veterans made so we could have it so good. A lot of people take that for granted. It drives me crazy when the national anthem is playing and people are talking or looking around. Sometimes it seems as though I am the only one paying attention and want to tell them to shut up. But preaching does no good—they have to learn for themselves what this country stands for, and what it took to get these freedoms.

I never did see combat. My closest chance was during the Branch Davidian situation in Waco, Texas, when there was talk of using our Army Ranger unit there.

When I joined my unit, everyone had combat experience from the Gulf War and other conflicts. But I didn't. I was the young platoon leader, and I had no experience in combat, yet the 40-year-old enlisted men had experience. They had to salute me and address me as "sir" and I was only 22. A lot of folks can't stand military academy graduates because there's a feeling that graduates think they know it all. I knew I didn't know it all. My first day with my unit, I met my sergeant.

"Good morning, sergeant," I said.

"Good morning, sir," he answered with a salute.

"Sergeant," I said, "I don't know squat. You will have to teach me everything."

That got things off on a good foot for us. That attribute of humility—and the people skills I have—all come from my father. That's the kind of person my dad is.

In the summer of 1993, I realized I didn't like my job. I was at Fort Benning, Georgia, on an officer basic course, sitting in a tank. At that time I knew Tim was in Hawaii pursuing his dream as he trained for the Ironman. When I talked to Tim on the phone the night before, he was so excited. I was living vicariously through him. There I was, in my fatigues in that big can (a tank) and it's always a hot day in fatigues in a tank in the middle of summer. We sat in that tank for five or six hours waiting for firing range clearance. That was when I decided to leave the Army.

But I knew I was giving up a lot. I had been in two years. But the Army opened up a window that allowed me to give up everything and get out right away with no strings attached. Basically, what happened was they had closed some bases and there were officers in Europe looking for stateside jobs in 1993.

It flew in the face of logic in a lot of ways to leave the Army. I had no job or anything waiting for me. Obviously, it was a big decision. I talked to Tim and then I got out of the Army. We were going to tour the nation and do triathlons, living for the training.

In a way, it was a good feeling. First of all, I was doing what I really wanted to do, and I had idolized Tim so much for making that choice for himself. Plus, I hadn't had any real time off since I entered West Point. I was ready to do something I wanted to do. I came home to Cedar Rapids, Iowa, and the first thing I did was to buy a bike. Tim went with me.

I did my first race a couple of months later. Tim and I made our first of many car trips, going to the Gulf Coast Triathlon in Florida.

We got a couple dozen bagels and Power Bars. We put the bikes on top of my Honda Accord and hit the road. We slept in the car a lot—we slept wherever we could. It sounds meager, but for the first time, I was really living.

The first trip was eventful. We were driving through Memphis, Tennessee, at 2 a.m. and a guy sideswiped my car. I think he was drunk. He gave us his license and insurance information, but as it turned out, he made it all up. I had to get the car fixed on my own.

But the Gulf Coast event itself was pretty cool. It was an age group race and we went against the pros. The water was really rough. We were all swimming together and, at the halfway point, a couple of the other guys didn't see the buoy. I did and turned, and at that point I was leading, ahead of all the pros. I had a slow transition from the swim to the bike and Tim and three of the pros caught up to me. I led for the first 35 miles of the bike race.

Disaster struck.

I had a flat tire. Usually, that's just a nuisance. But the night before, someone had stolen my pump. So I received a Did Not Finish (DNF). It was still promising, though. Tim qualified at the Ironman. It was bittersweet for me, because I had to watch Tim—whom I was very proud of—up on the dais. I was standing, just a face in the crowd, someone with a DNF. Despite that and the car accident, I thought, "Everything's cool. Finally, I'm happy."

From there, Tim and I went on a streak and for two years we went first and second place in almost every race we entered, both of us winning about half the time. Neither of us finished lower than second. That led us to be invited to the 1995 Pan Am Games qualifiers. The field was all professionals, but they still invited us.

Tim ended up getting a slot for the Games. I got pulled over for drafting in the bike race, which is illegal. But it was still exciting to be recognized as being top contenders in the sport.

Something else good came from that. We were starving athletes. We had no money when the DeGeorge Racing Team called. "We watched you guys, and we want to put you on our team," the guy said on the phone. I was ecstatic. Besides getting equipment, they paid for our travel to Europe and Hawaii, and we got to know the great pros on that team. Peter DeGeorge is a sweet, kind, generous, rich guy.

I struggled at times because of my inexperience. The first couple of years, when I saw gravel in the road I just plowed through it, sometimes resulting in a flat tire. I was still in the Army mentality, and I had to adjust. Plus, Tim and I had been water polo players, so my swimming needed work. It took me training and refining until 1998, when I finally started to feel like a real triathlete. Now, I'm not just a swimmer. My body developed from a swimmer's physique to one of a triathlete.

During the struggles, we always had long-term goals, a long-term timeline, and a long-term vision. It's fun to look back on it now and see the progress.

In 1996, Steve Lock of the U.S. Triathlon governing organization invited Tim and me to join the resident training team at the Olympic Training Center in Colorado Springs. It was the first year of the program, and Tim and I wanted to wait to see how it went the first year. Steve called again in 1997, and we moved to the OTC.

I will probably move to Boulder at some point to be with Tim. We will stay in the U.S. Triathlon organization, which helps us in countless ways.

We started training differently, doing more speed work. But we didn't want to give up our Ironman dreams. The Ironman differs from the Olympic triathlon. An Olympic triathlon is a .9-mile swim, a 24-mile bike ride, and then a 10K run. The Ironman in Hawaii is a 2.4-mile swim, a 112-mile bike ride and a regular marathon run—26.2 miles. The Ironman takes about nine hours, while the shorter length triathlons take fewer than two hours.

So we worked on training for both. Then, in 1998, things started out solidly. I had placed third in the 1997 World Cup and done well in international races. I realized I could do really well.

But then the most difficult thing I've ever had to deal with in my life happened.

I called my father every day. All four of his sons were very close to him. My father, Ken DeBoom, was an amazing man. People are destined to be certain things in life—a coach, a businessman, a teacher, whatever. We all have a God-given talent; Michael Jordan's for basketball, Van Gogh's for painting. My father's calling was to be a dad, and he was the best dad in the world. He was an insurance salesman. He was so good, he could sell snow to an Eskimo. In our hometown of Cedar Rapids, everyone knew my dad. He was a people person. He could walk into a room of 25 strangers and walk out with 25 new best friends. That's the kind of guy he was. We'd go to the gas station and the attendant knew him by name. We'd go to Dairy Queen and the person behind the counter would say, "Hi, Mr. DeBoom, the usual?" He'd call to order pizza and they'd recognize his voice.

Being an Iowan, he loved the Hawkeyes. He gave me Hawkeye football updates in the fall and basketball updates in the winter. Any sport the Hawkeyes were involved in merited an update.

Coming back from St. Croix on May 11, 1998, I called my dad from the airport before I boarded my plane to tell him how the race went. The phone rang and rang, and the machine picked up. But then my dad picked up the phone. I told him the race went fine. He said he was happy for me and he was looking forward to seeing me.

"How long till you're home?" Dad asked.

"About four hours," I said.

My father and I always ended our conversations telling each other "I love you." So he said, "I love you, Tony," and I said, "I love you too, Dad, and I'll call you when I get home."

When I landed in Colorado Springs, my big brother Todd was waiting for me.

"Dad died," Todd said.

My father had a heart aneurysm. My heart plummeted. My season plummeted. I stopped training and lost direction. The one good memory is that since the answering machine picked up and recorded our entire conversation, I still have it on tape. It means so much to have that, and the fact that I was able to tell him I loved him a final time.

My dad didn't care if we were athletes or what we did for employment. He just wanted us to be happy, and to spend time with us. He came to our event in Hawaii in 1997. He just wanted us to have fun and try out best. He was the pillar of strength in our family.

I decided not to do Ironman in 1998. But after Dad died, I went six weeks and did nothing. I decided I had to do something, or I'd have to call the year a washout. I decided to go to an Ironman qualifier in August 1998.

I started training like a madman. And then I had another setback. I broke my left arm at the elbow in a bike accident and had to wear a cast. I rode my trainer with the arm in a sling taped to my side so I didn't jiggle it. After two days, I convinced the doctor to put me in a soft cast so I could take it off. I started swimming in a couple of weeks. I was limited in what I could do, but I was working hard.

As it turns out, all I needed was a top-ten finish in Chicago to get into the Ironman. I ended up winning. It was the biggest victory of my life. All I could think about was my dad.

Ever since my father's death, Tim and I have been on a positive streak. Right after Chicago, I got on a plane to Japan and took fourth at the World championships. The trip itself was bizarre, going on planes, trains, and boats. But it was worth it.

I ended up going to Hawaii shortly thereafter and didn't do as well as I wanted, finishing 30th. Tim took 10th place. It picked up from there. I won the Pan Am qualifier in Tampa, Florida, which, aside from Chicago, was my biggest win. Tim then won New Zealand Ironman. Everything was just going incredibly well. And Tim and I know Dad is sitting up there in heaven, pulling a few strings to make sure his boys do well.

MARY JOE FERNANDEZ
TENNIS

Name: Mary Joe Fernandez
Sport: Tennis
Born: Aug. 19, 1971, Dominican Republic
Family: Parents, Jose and Sylvia; Sister, Mimi
Resides: Miami, Florida

Accomplishments: Most decorated U.S. Olympic tennis player ever; gold medal, 1996 Olympics, doubles; gold medal, 1992 Olympics, doubles; bronze medal, 1992 Olympics, singles

Hobbies: Golf, wave running, and water skiing

Post-Olympic goals and plans: Resumed pro tennis career after two Olympics

By Mary Joe Fernandez

In my tennis career, I've been very fortunate to play in the major events. But if I had to choose one thing that stands out, it would be the Olympic medals I won in 1992 and 1996.

When I was little, I didn't realize I had such an aptitude for tennis. I remember I could keep the ball going and I remember Chris Evert seemingly never missing a volley. I hit the ball back and forth to see how long I could do it. Fundamentals are the key to any sport and developing those shows a high level of concentration.

As children it seems we are always watching the Olympics on television. We seem to remember where we were during a particular Olympic moment, whether it was Mary Lou Retton winning the gold in gymnastics in or the USA hockey team taking gold in 1980.

So going to the Olympics as a competitor also gave me goose

bumps. I was honored to learn I had a shot at making the team, and then once I made it, there was a great sense of pride and accomplishment. And then, all of a sudden, I was there participating in the Opening Ceremony. I was with the top athletes from around the world, in all sports, not just my particular discipline.

Regardless of what a person has accomplished in his career, it is awe-inspiring to be among the best athletes in the world. We, as athletes, are usually big sports fans too, just like the spectators. So the awe of the spectators is shared by those of us who are competitors. We've watched these athletes on television and read about them, and it is meaningful to us to not only be counted among them, but to see them up close as well.

The opening ceremonies are a big part of a smaller picture. Every country, every sport, and every athlete has a particular story. Yet they all congregate during one brief period to put years, and perhaps lifetimes, on the line and fulfill the lifelong dream of being an Olympian.

To win the gold medal and hear the national anthem is one of those memories that will never leave me.

I love playing in the Federation Cup or anything else that involves being part of a team. Tennis is, just by its nature, an individual sport a lot of the time. But when you have teammates, you are playing for more than yourself. I feel a little more pressure under those circumstances, so it allows me to grow and develop different skills in different directions than from when, say, I am just playing singles events on tour. But I thoroughly enjoy the pressure of being a part of the team. My drive to excel is pushed by the fact that if I lose I will be letting down a lot more people than just myself. Plus, in the Olympics your medal is added to your country's medal count, so it is, once again, the small picture within the big picture that makes every Olympic moment not just inspirational, but meaningful to your national pride and the spirit of competition itself.

I've been able to experience a lot of fun and special moments in my tennis career. I credit a lot of that to my perspective, and that came from my parents. I had a really good upbringing because my parents emphasized values and morals. When it came to sports, the sportsmanship aspect was always number one. We were told that there would be no bad words or throwing racquets. Any temper tantrum or showing a lack of respect for opponents or referees was a ticket home and out of the sport. I've always had kind of a calm and low-key demeanor. But that temperament was honed and shaped by the solid upbringing from my parents, for which I am very grateful.

I love seeing kids at an event or a clinic. I believe parents or other family members should be role models for children. I also believe that athletes, actors, and other public figures have to realize that just by the nature of the media, they get a lot more attention than other people. With that attention comes a responsibility to conduct ourselves in a way that won't impact children in a bad way. We are fooling ourselves if we discard the role model status and say it's not our duty. While we don't raise other people's children, they do look up to us. That is more than enough motivation for me to always be cognizant of how my action can impact others. We do have that responsibility. The biggest impact we have is on the youth of this country. I enjoy giving autographs. It means a lot to know that I've accomplished something that these young people have taken notice of.

My career hasn't been without adversity. I've had to deal with injuries and other setbacks. But the combination of family and faith that I have has always made the tough times seem not so tough. When I go through adversity, it makes me stronger. I have to keep perspective and know everything happens for a reason. While those times make it difficult to see the big picture, I learn and grow from the setbacks and I am making that big picture even brighter.

At the French Open in 1993, I was so excited to be in the finals. Then losing, I felt so disappointed because I had thought, "I'm going to get my first grand slam." But the journey to that point was where I drew the most meaningful experience. In any experience, whether winning or losing, more goes into it than just the podium finish. Have I improved? Did I give my best effort? Did I see, win or lose, room for improvement? If the answer is "yes" to any of those, I came out a winner, regardless of what the final score was.

I also think education is very important. I didn't drop out of school because my family and I wanted me to have a "normal" childhood. I think the effect of that is positive in every way. First of all, education is invaluable. Secondly, it is where we learn the social skills needed in life. Also, don't look back and say, "Well, I've done a lot, but I wonder what it's like to go to a prom. I wonder what a pep assembly is like." Finally, all of those things will make us better professionals. We will be mature and ready to handle various things that come our way.

Being well rounded is important. Of course tennis is a huge part of my life, but I can't let it become my life. Then all of my hopes are in one hand, and what happens if those hopes are dashed? There's nothing left. Always have other options, and it's important to keep them open and pursue them on some level. I stayed in school until I was 17 and I didn't really play a lot of tournaments. I believed in pacing myself so I didn't force my body and mind to hold up day in and day out. Breaks are important as much mentally as physically.

I like playing doubles. It has really helped my singles because doubles has helped me play more aggressively. Through doubles I learned to close out points sooner. Of course, having a teammate can be a mental boost because it keeps me optimistic when things aren't going so well. So within your sport, or outside of it, find things and interests that will help as you pursue your passions.

I do think sports are important for kids. There are so many skills in sports that can be transferred into life, be it patience, sportsmanship, teamwork, or the determination to reach goals. Those all apply to any field. And in sports we have to keep moving forward, just as in life.

Sports teach wonderful life skills. Plus, some of the sports are great socially.

I've always taken the "team" aspect to mean the whole tennis tour. I'm not a big fan of controversy. I try to stay away from that and the confrontation, and what spurs those things on. There are not many people I don't like. I like to go with the flow and see the good in everyone. All the people I meet, even if they come across poorly or aren't well-regarded by others, can teach me something. Finding a way to get along with somebody who is difficult is making a big stride, and in turn that person will benefit from the association she or he has with you. That's winning in the game of life.

The thing I enjoy the most out of tennis is the competition. I like being out there trying to figure out how to win in a big-match situation. Over the years, the training has become tougher. But it's still fun. If you or your child aren't having fun, come home miserable from practice or dread to go, you should probably find another interest. Try new things. There's no telling what may pique your interest.

It takes a lot of time to get to the level of winning a Grand Slam or Olympic medal. The glamorous moments on television are a fraction of what went into simply getting to that point. It takes a lot of time and sacrifice. I get homesick easily, so I've had to spend a lot of time in airports and traveling. But I've always had fun and the sacrifice has been worth it. In addition to doing what I love for a living, I find great self-fulfillment and growth in it.

So enjoy the journey or the destination, regardless of whether that is first or last place.

YEWKI TOMITA GYMNASTICS

Name: Yewki Tomita
Sport: Gymnastics
Born: March 15, 1989, Tucson, Arizona
Family: Parents, Yoichi and Setsuko; sisters, Naomi, and Sakura
Resides: Tucson, Arizona
Trains: Gymnastics World of Tucson
Coach: Yoichi Tomita

Accomplishments: 1999 Winter Cup Challenge third place all-around (first, pommel horse); 1998 Winter Cup Challenge, second all-around; 1998 Goodwill Games bronze medalist pommel horse; 1997 International Junior Championships, third place all-around; 1997 John Hancock U.S. Gymnastics Championships, second place all-around

Hobbies: Other sports, piano

Post-Olympic goals and plans: Something to do with sports

By Yewki Tomita

From the stories I have heard, when I was younger, I didn't show a lot of potential in gymnastics.

I was a chubby, clumsy little boy at first. My dad owned a gym, so I was always running around and playing. But I wasn't a very coordinated little kid and I didn't have a lot of strength or ability.

I was fortunate to be taught by a great coach—my father. I was in my first competition when I was six years old. I competed with the seven- to-nine-year-olds. I wanted to see what it was like to compete. I didn't get great results. But I had a great time competing and it motivated me.

I wasn't a natural at the other sports I tried either. In middle school I tried basketball and of course we kids would always be outside playing football.

So pretty much everything I've been able to accomplish was through hard work. My dad has helped me, of course. But any success comes from my work ethic. I'm not the most talented guy out there or anything like that. But that makes each accomplishment that much more meaningful.

I know I haven't "made it" by any means in this sport. In the big picture I haven't done that much. But it's nice to be recognized by kids and give autographs. It means I'm headed in the right direction. This is what I've always dreamed of. I have to keep it going.

I've had to deal with injuries, but not too many. I had a compound fracture of my finger after doing a back toss in 1995. And I've had to work through a shoulder injury as well. The hardest challenge actually resulted from competition.

In 1997, I felt like I was on the verge of a breakout year. The 1997 USA Championships were in Denver. To qualify for that, I did very well in a regional qualifier, beating some big names in our sport. So I felt like I was ready to compete as a senior. I was convinced to compete as a junior. So I went into Denver expecting to win. I kind of faltered in Denver with all the lights shining. I took second place, but that was bad because physically I was ready, and thought I was by far the best.

I asked, "Why can I get second at regionals and totally mess up at a big meet?" It was all mental. Young people feel like they know everything. So being brought back down can be a good thing.

I think my personality is that if I fail, I'd better do it right the next time. I'm tough on myself that way. In Denver after the vault I just sat there. I remember thinking, "I don't want to feel this way ever again." It was a low feeling. I finished second, but the placing didn't matter because I hadn't performed. Winning is about more than receiving first place, it's about how we do, what we expect of ourselves, and how we put everything together. That experience, which seemed so devastating at the time, actually gave me more confidence when the 1998 season rolled around. I knew how bad it felt to be second, but I also knew that I could achieve first if I competed to the best of my ability.

Learning from mistakes is essential in gymnastics. I watch a lot of film, and I've seen guys mess up but come back to finish strong. My father always points those things out to me. "Look how he messed up but how good he finished." That's the mental part of the sport, and it is very important.

In this sport, patience is vital. That's especially true for me. I'm not one to try a trick and hit it the first time. I get frustrated in practice, but I will see it through. I'll overcome the obstacle and keep attacking until I get it right.

People have to realize that talent isn't the most important thing in our sport. At the lower levels, talent helps a lot. But once you get to be an elite and compete in the big time, everyone has that talent. So talent is not the determining factor. The largest part is mental. You see kids shine at the lower level, but then they don't make it to the next level. That's not because of talent; it's a matter of putting everything together mentally and having the focus, confidence, and concentration to make it happen.

I've always had the dream of making it to the Olympics. It wasn't one particular thing, but just being around the sport gave me the idea at six years of age that the Olympics would be the pinnacle.

When we are young, we set goals. When I first thought about going to the Olympics, I envisioned winning the all-around and even winning all events. Of course, now I realize that might not be possible for anyone to do. Yet there's still part of me that wants to do more than just compete. That's why I still don't feel like my accomplishments warrant much attention.

To me, it's a complete honor to go out and be able to represent America in any sport. After traveling around the world, I realize how lucky I am to live here, how fortunate to have been born here.

It's nice to hear people say that I come across as mature. To tell you the truth, if that's true, all the credit goes to my parents. Then again, if you ask my sisters at home, I'm not all that mature!

But I do try to take that to gymnastics. In competition, my style is to be calm, cool, and collected. If I do well or badly, I don't want to show too much emotion. That style doesn't work for everyone. For me, it's important that everyone finds a style that works for them. You can be outgoing and expressive or calm and show very little emotion. I don't think either style is good or bad; it's just a matter of a person finding his own style.

Everything relates to each other—sports to other sports, and sports to life. As far as the concentration and focus you have in gymnastics go, you need that in life. You have to be a competitor and want to win every time, whether it's on a mat or in an office.

It's important to work hard but enjoy what you are doing. To be honest, I don't really enjoy coming to practice at 7:00 in the morning and then working out a couple of hours and going to school and then coming back later in the day for another workout. In that way, training has really helped me with my time management skills.

I took a full load at the University of Arizona in 1998-99 and it was tough to balance all of my activities. I do know that gymnastics has helped me in school. After facing pressure, like at the Goodwill Games, I don't get fazed taking a big test in school. I have experienced pressure through competition, and it's helped me in life.

I love the competition because it motivates me to push myself through the tough, long workouts. I always keep that in the back of my mind. If I don't give 100 percent during training, whatever I win in competition won't be as meaningful and won't give a lasting sense of accomplishment. The training is 99 percent of the journey and usually the competition is merely a reflection of one's training.

One of the great things about my dad is that he's not a heavy-duty sports father who pushes me too much. He pushes me in the gym and that's great, it is what I need as an athlete, but he always wants it to be fun. We can have an intense workout and then go play a round of golf together. So we really enjoy each other's company, and I appreciate that because I know it's hard sometimes when a father coaches a son. I just have to credit him for that.

I have also learned that it's important to get away from the sport every once in a while. For some people, that means a couple of times a week, or just going out and having fun at least one night here and there. When I take a break, I come back to the gym refreshed. That's another great part about America—we have that attitude that we need to have fun with everything we do. I really have adapted to that idea. If I had grown up in China or another country, I might not have the attitude that I need to relieve stress and have some fun.

I don't know what the future will be like for me when I'm finished competing. I'll just leave my options open. I'd like to be a doctor and perhaps be in sports medicine so I can still be involved in gymnastics and sports.

We have a close-knit family. I know that whether I succeed big time or fail big time, I will have them behind me. They will be there to congratulate me or console me. It's good to know I have that behind me.

B.J. BEDFORD
SWIMMING

Name: Barbara "B.J." Bedford
Sport: Swimming
Born: Nov. 9, 1972, Hanover, New Hampshire
Family: Parents, Fred and Jane Bedford; Brothers, Fritz, Charles, and Ed
Resides: Colorado Springs, Colorado
Hometown: Etna, New Hampshire
College: University of Texas
Trains: Olympic Training Center, Colorado Springs
Coach: Jonty Skinner

Accomplishments: Two-time world champion on relays; seven-time U.S. national champion; Pan Am Games record holder; third-fastest American woman in 100-meter backstroke

Hobbies: Cooking, reading

Post-Olympic goals and plans: Marketing or advertising career

By B.J. Bedford

I don't remember learning how to swim. The water has been an integral part of my life longer than I can remember. I only know that there was water, I was in it, and it made me happy. I joined a competitive team at age five. They bent the rules and let me start before my sixth birthday because I had three brothers who also swam for Hanover. I maintain that it was my mother's exhaustion from chasing me up and down the bleachers at the pool that got me started.

By the time the 1984 Olympics rolled around, I had been on the team for six years and was quite an accomplished little fishy. I have a picture in my head of me sitting slack-jawed on the carpet in front of the television in the living room, watching my heroes, America's heroes, winning swimming events for God and country. It was watching those L.A. Games that kindled a tiny candle in my soul, and just like that, the fire of the Olympic dream seared my heart and began pumping through my veins. I turned and looked up to my mother, "Someday, Mommy, that's gonna be me."

Three short years later, I qualified for the Olympic Trials at my first junior nationals. So, in another year, I headed for a competition to pit myself against the very best, full of delusions of grandeur, determined to conquer the world. Needless to say, I missed the Olympic team by a mere 73 places, my high hopes crashing to the ground and leaving me temporarily crestfallen. But at 15, I could never stay down for too long and set about pestering my idols for autographs, finishing the competition as a spectator.

When I was entering my junior year in high school, my mom told me that I would be going to a new school, The Peddie School in Hightstown, New Jersey. A typical 15-year old, I knew my mother was dead wrong in that decision, and, duh, in most things.

Nevertheless, I went to the school, grudgingly and kicking and screaming the whole way. Years later, I was loath to admit my mother had been right, and sending me off was the best possible thing for me. I had started to lose interest in swimming, as it wasn't panning out to be all I had hoped, and so I decided that my social life was much more important. That difficult decision my mother made on my behalf was insightful and commendable. I can't begin to express the gratitude I feel toward her. At Peddie I met a man who became my surrogate father, Chris Martin. My dad wasn't really ever involved in my life. As time showed me, that was also probably a good thing, but that is another story.

Training at Peddie was unlike anything I had ever done. The kids at that school had an intensity the likes of which I had never seen, nor have I seen since. They worked so hard; I was scared to death. Initially, I felt like I had been sent to a bootcamp. My swim team at home had practice every day, but I seldom made more than five workouts a week and had never trained more than once a day.

These kids swam twice a day at least three times a week with no days off, not even Sundays. I was more or less pressured by the other kids to work hard, not the type of peer pressure that is normally found. Chris's mentality was that the hard work paid off later, like putting money in the bank. When I arrived I hid under the lane lines while everyone else was swimming. It was just too hard for me. The swimmers ignored me, assuming that I was a "scrub."

At the first or second meet of the season, I broke the school record in the 100-yard backstroke. All of a sudden everyone noticed me, but no one seemed to like what he saw. Chris actually forced Nelson Diebel to be my friend, because no one else would. Nelson didn't want to be my friend, but I think Chris threatened him or something. Actually, that one turned out well because to this day, Nelson is one of my best friends, despite our strained beginnings.

The worst thing I remember doing at Peddie was a three-hour straight swim wearing sneakers. I think I cried for the first hour, but I finished. In retrospect, I credit Chris Martin and the kids I went to school with for teaching me the value of hard work, and that with that work behind me, nothing is impossible. That is a belief that keeps my hope alive today.

I went to college in Austin at the University of Texas. I had a great four years. Each place I went had its lesson, and this one, like the others, was not easily learned. I swam for another control freak, (aren't all coaches, deep down?) Mark Schubert. He is an Olympic coach a few times over and I have a tremendous amount of respect and love for him.

I went to Texas after setting a high school record in the 100-yard backstroke, finishing third in, I think, three events at Nationals my senior year. I viewed myself as quite the little prospect. I was in for a big, fat chunk of humble pie in my first workout at the NCAA championship school. I got in a lane with Leigh Ann Fetter (American record holder at the time in the 50-yard freestyle), Erika Hansen (multiple Olympian), and Whitney Hedgepeth (also multiple Olympian). I thought I was pretty good, until I got my bottom kicked up and down the pool for an hour by those women and pretty much everyone else in the pool.

I left practice, went into the locker room, hid in a toilet stall, and cried. I didn't think I could offer anything to a team with all those amazing swimmers. I came from being a big fish in a relatively small pond, to being a freshman on a team that would later score more points at NCAAs than any in the history of women's swimming. Discouraged? I would say I was. Somehow, at 17, I couldn't stay down for too long, and I started to focus on what I knew I could do, backstroke. Mark told me he needed someone to swim butterfly, so I did that, vowing that at some point I was going to be the best backstroker Texas had ever seen. I applied my hard work ethic, and, by the end of my time at Texas, I held the school record. The moral of my college career? Never say die.

The Olympic Trials rolled around again during my college career, at the end of my sophomore year. I don't know if I've blocked it out, or I really can't remember, but I don't know exactly what went wrong. I think I had gained some weight, maybe ten pounds, and I had again allowed my focus to drift away from swimming and into my social life. I had a serious boyfriend and was beginning to establish an identity for myself, desperately wanting to be liked by everyone around me. I think I was stretched too thinly and not seeing the important things as being important.

What went wrong? I can't honestly say, but if I had to hazard a guess, I would say that I cultivated a fear of failure so large that it became a self-fulfilling prophecy. I thought about it all the time and could never bring myself to answer the question: What if I don't make it? What will I do? I could not answer the question because I didn't believe the answer: The answer was nothing. I go on, time moves forward, with or without me. I didn't understand that believing in failure gives it power over me. That was a decision I made at that time; I had faith in nothing, and that was what I got. Well, I got seventh place, which might as well have been seven hundredth place at that meet.

The most important lesson I took away from Texas was one of class, how to win and lose with dignity. It always seems to be easy to win, and easy to smile when everything is right there at my fingertips, but losing is another story. One of the hardest things in the world is to be bested by one of my peers when in my heart I believe I am the better swimmer. A little harder but even more necessary is to congratulate those who finish the race before me, replacing my own hopes for another day. Nobody said being a good sport was fun or easy, but if it were, everyone would do it. I learned that lesson, and it never gets any easier, but I recognize and appreciate it when others do it for me, and that's the reward.

I stayed at Texas to finish my schooling, another nine hours, and then decided to go back to Chris Martin. He had always found ways to push me to success. And I still loved him very much, as I do now. He was coaching then at the University of Florida in Gainesville, so I packed up my car, put a U-Haul behind it and set out for a new beginning. I knew I was pretty out of shape when I got there, although I had shown up on his doorstep a few summers before to train and had been way worse. So I got there, and placed my hopes and dreams in the hands of my high school coach, and asked him once again to take me to the promised land.

This is probably the toughest part for me to write about. I went into the Olympic Trials in 1996 as the No. 1 qualifier in the 100- and 200-meter backstroke events. I was, as much as anyone can be in our sport, a shoo-in to make the team. I had trained hard, I had done everything Chris had asked of me, and I wanted to make that team more than anything else in life.

Well, blunt and to the point, I didn't make it. I was the third fastest 100-meter backstroker in the country that year, the one year I needed to be first or second. There are a lot of technical things I can say about what happened, how many strokes I took, what my frequency of strokes was, but it all came down to being petrified. I was scared to death to do the one thing that I loved more than anything—race. My coach looked at me when I finished and shrugged. He didn't know what had happened and I didn't either for a long, long time. The Olympic Trials come around every four years, and I exaggerated their importance so much that it loomed above me in all things.

It was like a weight that I refused to acknowledge, pulling me down every day. From this meet, years later, I learned to face my fears. More often than not, they are irrational and without basis in fact. Was I afraid of failure or success? I think parts of me were afraid of both. There's always that irrational voice inside my head that screams that if I don't perform well, no one will love me. I listened too much to that voice, and not enough to my body and everything that I had put myself through to be the athlete that I am. It's OK for me to be afraid, I just can't be paralyzed by it.

So I left Florida. When I moved back to Texas, I wasn't the same person I had been. My confidence was gone, I had no direction, I didn't know what to do.

When the relationship with my boyfriend started to fall apart, I got a well-timed call from Jonty Skinner telling me that I had to try out for the resident team. He sounded like he was sure that I would do well there and that my career could be resurrected. I ran from my problems with my boyfriend and moved to Colorado.

I live in Colorado Springs, Colorado, now and have trained at the Olympic Training Center for two of the three years I've lived here. I must say that Jonty Skinner is a coach in whom I believe. He is someone who can move mountains, and I would follow him to the ends of the earth to witness the act. Despite all of my adoration for Jonty, and pretty much every coach I've had, my trials and tribulations have led me to take control of my destiny. If I work hard, I will do well. I have to be a good sport. And no one is responsible for my swimming but me, and I can't be afraid of that. It's part of growing up, which I hope I never cease to do.

I remember the winters in New Hampshire when I was a child. After a snowstorm, the ground became like a fresh gesso canvas, crisp and just waiting for an artist to create a picture. I was the first one to jump out into a fresh area of snow and gingerly step around to find the best spot, and pow! A snow angel! The tough part wasn't finding the perfect place; it was getting up and making the angel appear as if it had materialized out of thin air.

The next best thing to snow angels was being able to look behind me at the footsteps in the crisp clean snow, and to see how it materialized. What a marvelous concept, being able to look back on that blanket of snow where no one else's feet had trodden, that no one else could claim.

I used to walk a trail on the way to the bus stop as a little girl. I'm sure it was no more than a half a mile, but to my short young legs, it seemed like a million miles. On the way to school, my walk always went quickly, as it was all downhill. The hard part was trudging home afterward, up two hills, one along the road, the second a winding trail which ran into my driveway. I always dreaded that walk unless it had snowed all day while we were at school. It was only then that I could blaze my own fresh path, confident that my feet alone had made each mark.

On the way up the trail, I sometimes stopped to catch my breath when I got tired. I turned and looked behind me to see the path that I had left on my way. I can't explain the overwhelming sense of accomplishment that I could get from seeing the imprint of my tiny feet, each step that much closer to attaining my goal of the top of the hill.

I turned back to the task at hand, and renewed my efforts to get back to my house, to my mother's arms, ever loving, ever proud. I was excited to get to the warmth of our home, but I always turned to see how far I had come. These words have been just that for me. I've turned and looked at the meandering trail that I've blazed, with all the backtracking and pit stops along the way. This has been my journey, and the top is not far now. My shoes are bigger, my resolve is stronger, and I never dreamed that my little hill could evolve into the mountain that it has. But today is a step. And tomorrow is a step, and tomorrow and tomorrow.

It snows, it rains, and sometimes I think the wind will knock me off my feet. Sometimes there's something that I am afraid to let go of that holds me back. So I let go of my fear and take another step, because one day soon, the sun is going to rise and set on my mountain. That will be my day, the realization of my goal and my dream. I'll turn and reflect upon my footsteps, and then I'll cry, because I'll never forget what it felt like to be at the bottom looking up.

JAY HAKKINEN
BIATHLON

Name: Jay Hakkinen
Sport: Biathlon
Born: July 19, 1977, Kasilof, Alaska
Family: Parents, Yvonne and Brian; Brothers, Collin and Jared
Resides: Kasilof, Alaska
Hometown: Kasilof, Alaska
Trains: All around the world
Coach: Algimantus Shalna

Accomplishments: 1993 cross country junior national champion; 1997 world junior champion; 1998 Winter Olympian
Hobbies: Cooking
Post-Olympic goals and plans: College and a real life

By Jay Hakkinen

I began training at a crawl. I don't quite remember those early days, but if my mother's memories are correct, it was the beginning of a lifestyle that led me to my career as a biathlete. I didn't really think of it as training when driving home into the wilderness of Alaska. My brothers and I, like most brothers, would start fighting in the car, so my parents would make us get out and run the final mile or two home.

I started biking the 20 miles to my grandmother's house, not for training necessarily, but because Grandma had candy and cable television. I took care of intervals by running upstairs to reach the only locking door in our house before my brothers could practice wrestling moves on me.

Subconsciously, my sporting life was beginning and my family supported me the whole way. My oldest brother, Collin, was always trying new sports, which sparked Jared, my other brother, and me to follow suit. Jared was closer to my age and was often a teammate. He in particular helped push me to become better.

My two trailblazing brothers are also very hard workers, which helped me to avoid large amounts of work. My only exposure to work was one month each summer in Bristol Bay while commercial fishing with my family. Beginning when I was seven, we were dropped off at a decrepit hunting cabin by bush plane and greeted by mosquitoes. During that month we caught sockeye salmon by the thousands, or none at all, depending on the mood of the fish. The lack of sleep and manual labor made me realize I was meant for the athletic life.

The first sport my family led me to was ice hockey. I became as passionate about it as Wayne Gretzky. However, my passion could not overcome a slight lack of talent. I was a decent player, but only because of the talents which make me a competitive biathlete. When I realized I didn't have the qualities to be a standout player, I became dissatisfied. I discontinued my hockey ambitions for cross-country skiing, which I knew I could do well.

Cross-country skiing came to me naturally. A junior national victory in my first competitive year of skiing confirmed I had found a sport in which I could succeed. I quickly became a skiing enthusiast, followed the top skiers, and began studying how I needed to train.

My skiing enthusiasm led me to Vingrom, Norway. I went on a foreign exchange, which was another hand-me-down tradition from my brothers. I lived with the Ostengen family, who kindly arranged for me to train with the biathlon club. I borrowed a rifle for the shooting portion, and happily trained for biathlon. However, I still held on to my enthusiasm for skiing, which I have traces of to this day.

My desire to become the best made it clear biathlon was the sport that would guide me to my full potential as an athlete. At the time the U.S. Biathlon Association was in a period of transition. It wasn't getting the results it wanted and decided to put the focus on winning a gold medal in the 2002 Olympics. It wanted to bring young juniors up through the program and then breed them into gold medalists. The program's goals were the same as mine.

The shooting element of the sport was relatively new to me, and since I had been in biathlon races with a head-down-don't-think cross-country mentality, I found the shooting difficult. As I continued to train, I became obsessed with overcoming the challenge of biathlon.

I have taken several significant steps toward my ultimate goals, but my past results mean very little beyond showing my future potential. However, the more I achieve, the prouder I am of the accomplishments that got me where I am. In my first competitive year as a biathlete, at age 16, my 40th place at the world junior championships was the top American finish. In 1995, I took ninth place at world juniors, which sparked a hope that I could compete internationally. The next year I won America's first international gold medal at a Europa Cup race in Russia, which I followed up with another gold and bronze medal that same year, confirming my confidence in the sport.

At the 1997 world junior championships, my last year as a junior, I confidently felt I was the guy who was supposed to win, and I raced according to my confidence. Unfortunately, my weakness in the range pushed me down to a disappointing ninth, the same result I had had two years previous. The next day I changed to a more conservative race strategy, learning from my failure, and I finished with a world junior gold medal.

With my junior years expired, I started my first year as a senior by competing in the 1998 Winter Olympic team. I remember hearing former U.S. Nordic ski team coach John Estle say that an athlete's first Olympics is just for the experience. That turned out to be true. I was just 20 years old, which is very young for an Olympic biathlete, but at the same time, my goal was to put a perfect race together so I could medal.

Realistically, I had been in the top 25 in only one World Cup prior to the Olympics. My competition was skiing 90 seconds faster than I, and I was still struggling with my standing shooting. I thought when the 10K was canceled it was a second chance for a miracle to happen. But, instead, it indicated even more forcefully that no miracle, luck, or probability was going to win me a medal. I would have to work for it. In summary, my learning experience resulted in a 63rd and a 42nd place.

I did everything I could to succeed in Nagano, but in trying I learned what it would take to win an Olympic medal. With success and failure, experience and experimentation, I continue. I am proud of my accomplishments, but if I retired right now, they would all lose their luster. That is because they were all just steps toward where I wanted to go when I began: To be the best. The closer I get toward that goal, the prouder I am of what I have accomplished.

Looking to the future, I will compete against approximately the same people as I did in Nagano, and in every World Cup and world championship leading up to the next Olympics in Salt Lake City. There is no higher level. If I want to become the best, I now know whom I have to beat.

For this reason, I've always stayed focused on the international circuit. I have little concern for my results nationally. I race as well as I can at nationals, but I want to compete against the best in the world.

My lackluster national focus almost backfired at the 1998 Olympic Trials. I won the first race at the trials but the following two races were near disastrous performances. Going into the last race there were about ten people who could have made the team because the point standings were so close. I put a decent race together and took third place, enough to make the team. However, having it come down to the last race was stressful and humbling.

Biathlon in itself is a humbling sport. There is great respect on the international circuit, since everyone has races where something goes wrong, whether it's shooting, skiing, or any of a variety of circumstances. It is the biathletes against biathlon, and as we try to conquer the sport, we can rejoice when someone succeeds. That makes it a pleasant atmosphere to compete in, and a difficult sport to dominate.

My dedication toward the sport has meant making sacrifices, but I have received rewards in return. I'm making the progress I need, strengthening weaknesses such as my standing shooting, and I am gaining confidence from my results. The more I train the more I become focused and intense about being the best. I put everything else in my life aside or on hold. So there's nothing really to move me away from those goals. I get on the road sometimes and I think, "I have thousands of miles and thousands of hours to go," and it's mind-boggling, but there's no reason to stop, either.

Although I am doing everything in my power to succeed in biathlon, I made one clear rule for myself when I began the sport—I would not artificially enhance my performance. I do not want any credit to go to performance-enhancing substances. I have stood firmly by that standard. It means I have to weigh down my plate with substantial servings of food, but I have never felt that has been a disadvantage. I hope to prove to myself, the other athletes, and future athletes, that an organic human being can achieve greatness.

I also hope that what I've done will help biathlon gain exposure, especially in the U.S. Although every sport can be mocked as ridiculous by those ignorant of its purpose, fortunately biathlon justifies itself quite well. Biathlon was originally a way to hunt. Cave drawings in Norway depict a man with a bow and arrow on skis.

This is a sport that tests an entire person. Cross-country skiing is among the most physically demanding sports, and shooting is among the most mentally demanding. I like to joke that I do well because I am a dull person, and there is some truth to that. The long training hours and emotionless focus create an environment I thrive in. It is a sport with so many variables that it brings out the weaknesses in everyone.

That gives me a constant challenge. It has humbled me many times, which makes me want to conquer it all the more, which keeps me pursuing the impossible.

ERIKA LYNN BROWN
CURLING

Name: Erika Lynn Brown
Sport: Curling
Born: Jan. 25, 1973, Madison, Wisconsin
Family: Parents, Steve and Diane Brown; Brother, Craig
Resides: Northbrook, Illinois
Hometown: Madison, Wisconsin
Trains: Madison Curling Club, Chicago Curling Club
Coach: Steve Brown

Accomplishments: Curling: Six world junior championship appearances; three world junior medals; three women's world championship appearances; two world silver medals (1996, 1999); Winter Olympics appearances (1988, 1998); 1996, 1999 USOC Olympic Curling Team of the Year; 1989, 1994 USOC Female Curling Athlete of the Year

Hobbies: Golf, tennis, biking

Post-Olympic goals and plans: Work as a physician assistant, continue to stay involved in the sport of curling

By Erika Lynn Brown

My dad enrolled me in every sport league he could find—soccer, Little League baseball, track and field, golf, ice skating, and of course, curling. My parents didn't have to convince me to like curling. I grew up around it, and it was never a matter of if I was going to play, but rather, when could I start.

My first trip to a curling club was as an eight-day-old. My dad was playing in a Milwaukee Bonspiel (weekend tournament) and my mother, new to parenthood, figured hauling the sleeping babe to the club would be a harmless gesture. Little did she realize that she would never be able to drag me away.

I virtually grew up in the Madison Curling Club. Old-timers at the club surely remember the bratty Brown kids hanging out a few nights a week while their parents curled in the "mixed" couple leagues. A curling stone weighs 42 pounds, too much for a spindly seven-year-old like me to handle, so we improvised. Ashtrays were my make-shift curling stones until the day I shattered one across the ice. After that I had to resort to tissue boxes until I gained a few more pounds and years.

As soon as I was big enough to deliver the real stone 140 feet to the opposite end of the sheet of ice, I started playing in the women's leagues as a young girl. In middle school I gathered up a group of friends and my dad arranged for us to play in a high school curling league in some of the small towns north of Madison. It was like a weekly field trip. We belted out songs the whole way to the match and then without a care in the world we gave the high schoolers a run for their money.

Undoubtedly, my dad realized the importance of playing against the more experienced teams. A few years later I teamed up with some of those early competitors and begin playing on a national level.

To say that our family is involved in curling is a bit of an understatement. My parents have owned a nationwide curling supply business for 20 years. Our house has been described as a museum with everything from curling stone plant holders to Olympic pin collections to the oversized curling stone painted on the garage door publicizing our obsession to our customers and neighbors. Our family vacations revolve around the annual national championship in such glamorous locations as Bismarck, North Dakota, and Hibbing, Minnesota, in the deep of winter.

Nevertheless, we always have an excuse to spend time together. Luckily the whole family is equally devoted to the sport. My brother Craig is a successful curler in his own right. One of the most memorable championships was my last world junior appearance in Sophia, Bulgaria. My brother was representing the U.S. on the junior men's team. We shared information about the ice conditions and, perhaps more importantly, the location of American-style pizza parlors. Both of us ended up on the podium.

My dad has been my coach from the beginning. With my mother "spotting" we have become excellent acrobats walking the tightrope between dad/coach and daughter/athlete. He is a very dedicated athlete and coach and has instilled his own work ethic in me. He made certain I developed strong fundamentals, entered me in the top competitions, and constantly challenged me to improve. He is available to practice with me day or night, and while he says he has taught me everything he knows about the game, he still manages to routinely beat me at one-on-one.

My competitive spirit developed at an early age. We had more than 50 baseballs and the entire family went to the ball diamond each night so my brother and I could take extra batting practice. I was determined to beat out the boys and earn a spot on the all-star team. Dad pitched, mom shagged, and Craig and I hit balls until the moon was brighter than the sun.

Golf followed the same principle. Wisconsin high school girls' golf is played in the fall, which can seem like winter in the northern Midwest. I sometimes hit balls before school, and then stayed after regular practice in the afternoon to hit another bucket. A few nights a week after supper Dad and I would zip back to the course to squeeze in another hour of practice. There were times when it was snowing and so unbelievably cold that we would keep the car running with the heater on full blast so that I could jump in after every dozen balls and thaw out my fingers and toes.

Toward the end of those sessions I started rolling my eyes and let out one of those patented daughter whines "daaaAAAaadddd!" pretending this was torture. But I was the one who insisted on staying until I finished on a solid, straight shot. The final day of the state tournament there was an hour delay waiting for the snow to melt off the first tee. This didn't phase me a bit and I went on to win the tournament.

All of this exposure to cold weather made me a perfect

candidate for Big Ten women's golf. I played for the University of Wisconsin under Coach Tiziani, a very skilled, matter-of-fact, shoot-74-for-me-and-I'll-buy-you-an-extra-plate-of-gnocci kind of guy. While he may not have understood all of the intricacies of curling, he knew what it meant to be captivated by a sport and recognized that competition at a top level in one sport will only make you tougher in another. As even the weekend golfer knows, golf requires much patience and precision. The skills I learned on the course certainly have contributed to my mental toughness on the ice.

Our college golf season is played in the fall. The spring and every day in between are spent on the ice with my curling team. I learned early on how to balance my schedule to make room for practice, school, and the occasional social outing. My boyfriend, Mika, and I started dating in college and I will never forget the first night we went to dinner with my family at our favorite restaurant, Paisans. The topic of curling came up within seconds as is customary with my family. Five minutes into the conversation I could tell he hadn't understood a word we had said. With all of the terminology, names of fellow curlers, and a lifetime of competition history, it became instantly clear that he would have to learn this new language or we were going to have a heck of a time communicating. He was a natural on the ice and soon enough was questioning my game strategy and winning state competitions. Welcome to the family!

As a child, the Olympics transfixed me. When I wasn't glued to the television watching the events I was busy assembling scrapbooks of the newspaper articles on my favorite athletes and making gigantic Olympic ring replicas for my bedroom wall.

When the flyers announcing the Olympic Trials for curling's debut as a demonstration sport in the 1988 Calgary Olympics were posted, my father's mind immediately started spinning, "Wow, what an opportunity for Erika to get some valuable experience against the top U.S. women curlers." Lisa Schoeneberg had played at a previous national championship with my mother, and Dad thought she was the best of the locals, so she was enlisted first.

What we lacked in experience we made up for in enthusiasm. Dad said that we could beat anyone, and who were we to know any better. This served us well as we astonishingly rolled through the state and national trials to win the coveted Olympic berth. Now what? Four young Wisconsin girls going to the Olympics with zero international experiences. Well, good ol' Dad had a plan: practice, practice, practice at 6 a.m. before school, before lunch breaks, after school, before leagues, or 10:30 at night when the leagues finished up.

We secured the support of the University of Wisconsin volleyball coach, Steve Lowe, to work with us on sports psychology. Dad knew the impact these games could have on our young lives and took no shortcuts. He took a leave of absence from a 17-year job to work with us every step of the journey.

It certainly wasn't instant success. Our first taste of international competition came at a four-day tournament in Saskatoon, Saskatchewan. We were quickly eliminated after losing three in a row and it was clear we had work to do. We went to Calgary a few months before the Olympics to play in another tournament and acclimatize to the city and Olympic hype. How did we fare this time? A local headline summed up our status: "Yanks Still Learning!" It stressed the positives, slowly removed the intimidation factor, and we continued to progress.

At the games themselves, we played superbly. It wasn't the Cinderella story where we won the medal, but we came oh-so-close. After beginning the week with three tough losses, we concluded the round robin with a thrilling victory over the former German world champions giving us a 4-3 record and a spot in the tiebreaker for the medal round. We lost a heartbreaker to the Norwegians. The same sports writer who had proclaimed "Yanks Still Learning" months earlier now proclaimed, "Never have I witnessed the maturing of such a young team so rapidly. They will be a force in the future world events." I did not have my medal, but I did gain the belief that I could compete against the world's best and that would fuel my motivation for years to come.

Ten years later, curling became a medal sport and was to make its debut in Nagano, Japan. Three out of the four players on the team had been together since 1988 and by this time our expectations revolved around the hardware. The week of the Olympic Trials in Duluth, Minnesota, in December 1997 was the most grueling week in my competition history. Lisa and I would lie in our hotel room each night just waiting for the other person to give off a big sigh signaling that it was okay to start talking or deal the cards for double solitaire because insomnia had overcome us again. We ended the five-day tournament with a 9-1 record and a trip to Japan. It was a moment of anticipation, validation, and exhaustion.

As we entered the stadium for the Opening Ceremony I was bursting with pride. I was representing the United States, I was marching in with my longtime teammates and parents close by, and I was part of a moment in history for the sport of curling.

The Olympics will never cease to be an awe-inspiring event for me. However, returning to the Olympics for a second time changed my focus. No longer was I an awe-struck teen-ager obsessed with trying to look cool in my USA clothing allotment and hoping we would win a game. My team and I were on a mission. We felt like we were the most prepared of our lives. Well, after three losses in a row I was back to hoping we would win a game! It was a frustrating week in the foothills of Japan. We ended the competition tied for fifth place. I was reminded that there are no guarantees in sports. Training harder than your competitors certainly will give you the edge, but it is taking advantage of all of your opportunities during the battle that will make you a champion.

Our team dissolved after the Olympics. We had accomplished a great deal together over 10 years, yet each of us was tired and in need of rejuvenation. I was fortunate to join forces with a new skip and some old friends/teammates. The chemistry is amazing, considering that we live in four different states. It wasn't the convenience I was accustomed to in Madison where the whole team had lived within a five-mile radius of one another.

My new team qualified for the 1999 world championships in St.

John, New Brunswick. Now, this certainly wasn't the Alps of Europe, nor was it in front of the home crowd, but for a curler it was heaven. The stands were sold out for each game all week long. Curling fans arrived in droves from all across Canada to cheer on the home favorites. Three games a day were broadcast across the country with viewership out-ranking the NHL. What joy to wake up in the morning, roll over in bed, flip on the television and see the best men's teams in the world playing the early draw.

Some may argue that a curling match might put them right back to sleep, but for me it was invigorating. The Canadian women dropped out of the hunt early and, being the underdogs to the south, we were adopted as the local favorites. All of the support from home and the stands wasn't quite enough for us to pull out a victory in the finals. We lost to Sweden and they became the first team to win four world titles. While we were disappointed, the season refreshed me.

The journey, at times tumultuous, at times thrilling, has filled me with dreams, confidence, humility, and vitality. I foresee plenty more opportunities for success, and, with a little luck, the first gold medal for the United States in curling.

BOBBY BREWER SWIMMING

Name: Bobby Brewer
Sport: Swimming
Born: Jan. 9, 1974, Atlanta, Georgia
Family: Parents, Jane and Larry Brewer; Sister, Karen McCarthy (Olympic Trial qualifier in same event)
Resides: Newport Beach, California
Hometown: Forest Park, Georgia
Coach: Dr. Dave Salo

Accomplishments: 1999: gold and silver medals at Phillips U.S. Spring Nationals, 100m backstroke; silver medal at Phillips U.S. Summer Nationals, 100m backstroke; gold medal at the U.S. Open, 100m backstroke; earned spot on U.S. Pan Pacific team; 1998: silver medalist at World University Games, 100m backstroke; NCAA, fifth place, 100-yard backstroke; Phillips 66 Summer Nationals, fourth place, 100m backstroke; 1995: bronze medal at World University Games, 100m backstroke; 1994: NCAA bronze medalist, 100-yard backstroke; bronze medal at Phillips 66 Summer Nationals, 100m backstroke; silver medal at U.S. Open, 100m backstroke; ranked sixth in the world

Hobbies: Surfing

Post-Olympic goals and plans: Interested in coaching and have the all-American entrepreneurial bug

By Bobby Brewer

I was excited as the 1994 fall swimming season approached. I had had a really good year the season before at the University of Georgia with a couple of Southeastern Conference titles.

I was coming off a great sophomore year at the University of Georgia and was on a roll with competitions and was turning heads in my training sessions leading into the summer of '94. About halfway through the summer I went to Fort Lauderdale, Florida, to train under the guidance of coaching legend Jack Nelson. My goal was to make the U.S. world championship team. But about halfway through the summer I began to have pain in my back and down my leg. I had experienced muscle strains and hamstrings in the past and thought that was my problem.

With the help of Coach Nelson I was guided to an exceptional massage therapist, chiropractor, and physical therapist. The problem was under control at the time, or so I thought, but I was spending most of my time out of the pool lying in bed on muscle relaxants and painkillers. A physician suggested I try a cortisone shot to speed up the healing process.

I went to world championship trials and swam fine in the morning. I qualified third with an easy swim, knowing I could go much faster in the finals. But between prelims and finals I had pain in my back that made its way into my left leg. The pain was worse than ever. I struggled with doctors and a massage therapist for the majority of time between prelims and finals of the 100 backstroke. But I felt strongly about the race and chose to swim regardless of the pain.

That night at finals after a very limited warm-up session, I isolated myself and attempted to block out the pain mentally. When it came time for the race I had changed my focus from the pain to the task at hand—making the world championship team. I knew they only took two people in each event and I had to be first or second behind world record holder Jeff Rouse. I had a great first 50. I was second at the wall and closing in on the leader. I was right where I wanted to be.

But 60 meters into the race I began to experience the back and leg pain again. It only made me push harder and, at the 75-meter mark, I lost control of my left leg as it sank in the water against my will. I pushed on with everything I had, kicking with only my right leg, and finished to the wall with all my heart. When I looked up at the scoreboard my name flashed up third. I had taken third place, although they only take the top two for the world championship team. I had missed making the team by three one-hundredths of a second, a nearly immeasurable distance. I was devastated with the outcome, but was more concerned that I could not control my left leg and that I was in a great deal of pain.

I tried to climb out of the pool, but my left leg wouldn't move. As I pulled myself from the pool my left leg collapsed under me and I fell to the deck of the pool. I was afraid, in horrible pain, and devastated from the outcome of the race.

An MRI showed a bulging disk. It hadn't ruptured at that point, but the strain from training and competitions had taken its toll. The doctor suggested complete rest for three months.

Now, on the swimming front there was some good news. I had qualified for the Pan Am Games team. So I thought, "This won't be a complete loss. I'll have to miss the college season but I can be back in February for the Pan American Games."

So I took three months off and returned to the doctor again. This time I had all the same complaints, yet the symptoms were getting worse. The doctor suggested cortisone shots and another three months off. Once again neither suggestion seemed to work and I returned to seek the advice of another doctor. He presented me with the same bad news and also asked me to take another three months off. At this time I was beginning to give up all hope and it was now too late to salvage the season for the Pan Am Games. I withdrew from the team, which was the final blow that took me over the edge.

I was frustrated and had given up on medicine, therapy, shots, etc. I couldn't take it any more and decided I had had enough. I was going to swim, pain or no pain. I went to the pool and did a practice on my own. It turned out to be a devastating mistake I will never forget.

I woke the next morning in excruciating pain and could not move my left leg. I tried to get out of bed. My right foot went forward but my left leg was limp and lifeless. I fell to the floor. Two days later I was put in emergency surgery in Atlanta. My doctor assured me everything would be fine.

After the surgery my first question was, "When will I swim again?"

I had chosen this particular surgeon because, while he told the truth, he was not overly pessimistic, as most doctors had been. He said, "You might not swim at the same level as before, but you may certainly try and I wish you the best of luck. But I have some bad news. There were complications in the surgery. The condition of the disk had worsened over the previous three months and had ruptured. The nerve in your spine has been cut off completely for some time. It has been completely damaged. It will heal at the rate of around one inch per month."

I did the math in my head: The nerve ran from my lower back all the way to my toes, about 4 feet. At 48 inches of nerve I was looking at four years until I would be completely recovered.

I gave up on everything. I dropped out of school. I was bedridden for three months and unable to move from my room. I gave up completely on the idea of swimming. I was done. I had nothing to look forward to and was as low as I could possibly be. The one thing I truly loved had been taken away from me and there was nothing I could do about it.

I had become a miserable person to be around, though my friends stopped by to check on me and my parents stuck by me through it all. I felt helpless and angry. I turned to painkillers and muscle relaxants for relief. I was headed for destruction.

One day in my third month of wallowing in self-pity I was in bed thinking of how miserable I was. At the time I had trophies placed around the room and plaques hanging on the walls. Well, one of the plaques came loose, fell from the wall, and smacked me in the head. This was it! I had had it. Nothing more could possibly go wrong.

I picked up the plaque and was ready to hurl it across the room. I started to heave it when I noticed it was a plaque my mother had made for me to commemorate the first national record I had broken.

The significance was not the place I finished, or the time I had gone, or even the fact that it was a national record. The significance was the memories I had of that day and the friends and family who supported me in achieving that goal.

The completion of the goal was not that significant; the fun I had and the path I took to achieve the goal were what I remembered. I thought, "What did I swim for? What did it all mean?" I decided that I swam because I loved the challenge of setting a goal, and, more importantly, I loved the fun and the experiences I had had on the way to achieving those goals. So in May 1995 the flame was rekindled in my heart and I set out to turn my life around. I wanted to swim again and I wanted to finish school.

That day, I got out of bed and went to the pool. I saw my age group coach who had always been a positive influence in my life and I asked him if he would coach me until I was able to get back into school. He agreed. On my first day I did one lap, which was the hardest lap I had ever done. At this point I knew it would be harder than I had expected. But the next day I went back and I did two laps, then three the next day and four the day after that. I kept building for the next few weeks up to a mile a day.

My doctor had warned me, "No starts or turns yet as they would put too much strain on your healing back." At this point I was a recreational swimmer in terms of what I could do. But in my mind I was on a mission. I had set the lofty goal of competing in just one more nationals and then I would be satisfied and could move on in my life. I had a one-track mind and at the time I don't remember feeling challenged at all. My motto was, "Nobody can stop me, not even my own body."

It was late June and I wanted to go to nationals at the end of July. A lot of people had written me off as crazy and had forgotten the name Bobby Brewer. However, I wanted to see my friends and be a part of the experience of a national championship meet. At that point, I went back to school and trained at the University of Georgia. I told them I would be back to swim, but because I had dropped out the previous year I had to walk on to make the team.

I went to nationals in July 1995 for my first race in more than a year. My doctor had released me to do "only enough starts and turns to get you through your races." By no means did I post a best time, but I shocked everyone by qualifying for the World University Games in Fukuoka, Japan. The question was, could I accept to go? Could I make it through a 15-hour plane ride in my condition? What would my doctor say about that? He wished me his best, and said it would be tough, but that I should give it a go.

Well, just as we expected, the plane ride gave me all kinds of trouble. The team doctor did everything he could to help me, but when we arrived I was in a great deal of pain. I was unable to train before my competition, but I managed to keep my hopes alive for a medal in my first international event in more than four years.

I managed a bronze medal; however, after the swim I was once again forced into a couple of weeks of complete bed rest. I was happy though. I had gone above and beyond my own goals, and more importantly, I was thrilled with the experiences I was blessed with.

This gave me the motivation to continue to set higher goals. I returned to school to compete for the University of Georgia swim team. I couldn't do any weight training and my water training was very limited. However, I was voted captain for both my remaining years, which kept my motivation high and my goals geared toward the team. I didn't do anything spectacular, but I finished a decorated career and got my degree.

After my last college championship meet I wanted to compete in just one more meet: the 1998 spring national championships. This next swim would decide the fate of my career. Would I move on to other interests or continue to pursue my Olympic dream?

That was the deciding point in my career. I won my first national championship and achieved my highest world ranking to that point. It ranked me sixth in the world. I would continue swimming.

At this point I moved to Irvine to train with the sprint guru, Dr. Dave Salo. He taught me about how the body works and how it reacts to exercise. We developed a plan in which I would be able to train at a high intensity level without affecting my back. That year,

1998, I took second at summer nationals, which ranked me fifth in the world. It also qualified me for the United States swimming national team, which would compete in the Olympic pool in Australia the following year in the Pan Pacific Championships.

There were a lot of ups and downs to get to that point. The summer of 1998 was the best I had in more than four years. Exactly four years after my devastating disappointment of not making the world championship team, I returned to the same meet. This time I qualified for the team, and this time there was no pain, only joy.

I proved a lot to myself by surpassing the goals I had set the day the plaque came crashing down onto my head. In retrospect I suppose that plaque knocked some sense into me. I have now changed my goals and my focus has turned to the 2000 Olympic Games in Sydney.

Looking back, the recovery after the surgery was far more mental than physical. It was mind over matter. I cursed the injury at the time, but now I almost think of it as a blessing. I wouldn't be where I am now without it. It has changed my views in so many ways and made me cherish what I have.

I love to talk to people about what I have endured. I learned about who I am and about life in general. The number one lesson from all this was to appreciate what I have. The adage about "not knowing what you have until it is gone" certainly rings true. I appreciate my health, the body I have been given and have learned the importance of taking care of it and respecting it. A person only gets one chance at making it the best it can be.

I appreciate the support from family and friends, and I cherish them. They played the biggest role in keeping my spirits high. Secondly, I realized I have to have fun with what I am doing. If I'm not having fun, I am not really experiencing it for what it is worth. Finally, there are always times in any endeavor when it seems easier to quit, and it may seem impossible to see the "big picture." However, if we love what we are doing, we stick with it. The reward will be overwhelming and, in retrospect, the ride to get there will be remembered as the most fun.

I did a lot of reading while I was bedridden. I read success stories. There was a common thread in them. At some point everyone who succeeds has overcome something that tested not only his abilities, but also the nature of his soul and the very fabric of his character. Michael Jordan was cut from his basketball team in high school. What if he had quit?

Until my injury I never dealt with adversity. Everything was golden for me to that point. I was a good swimmer and had done everything I had set my mind to accomplish. It almost seemed easy. It's the challenges of life that establish a person and define what he is truly made of. It is these challenges that make life interesting and worth living.

I cannot reiterate enough that everything can be taken away at any given moment. This idea helped me realize that swimming should not be stressful. It is something I enjoy. Making a team or setting a record now means more to me because of this perspective. I used to think it was a right of mine to be a great swimmer. Now I realize it is a privilege. I see kids who complain throughout practice and don't allow themselves to enjoy the experience. To achieve what we set out to achieve requires a good attitude and perspective and with that comes a meaningful experience.

Many people see me now as a sort of reference for injury or adversity. They know I am not afraid to talk about my vulnerability and that I am ready to offer support.

I view injuries differently these days. I used to see them as a weakness or excuse, but now I realize the physical and mental challenges adversities place before a person. I also realize the importance of adversity in developing a successful and truly complete and happy person. I know that, if approached the right way, these seemingly negative situations can be turned into something far more positive than you could have ever imagined. Never give up.

LINDSAY DIANNE BENKO SWIMMING

Name: Lindsay Dianne Benko
Sport: Swimming
Born: Nov. 29, 1976, Elkhart, Indiana
Family: Parents, Roger and Dianne; Sister, Lesley
Resides: Los Angeles, California
Hometown: Elkhart, Indiana
Trains: Southern California
Coach: Mark Schubert

Accomplishments: Five-time NCAA champ; two-time USA swimming national champ; member of USC national title team in 1997; holds numerous USC records on relays and individual; member of USA swimming national team; world champ member in 1998 and Pan Pacific member in '97 and '99; national team captain in '99; USC team captain '97- '98 and '98-'99

Hobbies: Going to the beach and movies with friends. I would like to learn how to surf.

Post-Olympic goals and plans: Continue swimming or working in public relations in Chicago

By Lindsay Dianne Benko

In Indiana, where I grew up, swimming is a big sport.

I started swimming at our country club in the summer league when I was six years old. I started year round at the YMCA when I was eight. I won my first state title at age 9, my first junior national title at 13, and senior national title at 21.

I started to concentrate solely on swimming when I entered high school. We had a really good team. In some states, swimmers compete in clubs, instead of for their high school. But in my hometown of Elkhart it was a big deal for us to win the Indiana State highschool championship.

In high school and in my younger years of swimming, my parents supported and encouraged me to take a break or relax. It turned out to be a key to keep me interested and motivated in the sport. Every high school spring break I went on vacation, whereas a lot of swimmers couldn't imagine taking a break at that time of year. I'm really glad that I did because I always came back feeling better. And it's important to keep having fun and keep life well balanced.

That balance has kept me in the sport. I participated in many school functions. I went to high school games and had a social life outside of swimming. Actually, my best friends weren't swimmers. I wasn't bombarded with swimming when I was younger. I think that helped keep my progress consistent.

My family always supported me. My dad played baseball in college so he understands the demands on a college athlete. He always told me to take a step back and enjoy it. My mom told me to always keep everything in perspective. So my parents were a huge influence on me. My sister always helped me with the having fun part of my life.

High school swimming was a blast even though I wasn't improving as much as I would have liked. I was still winning state championships and that was the main focus. The goal of being an Olympian had to be eased to the back of my mind because it really didn't look realistic. So I lowered my standards to being a regular progress swimmer. I was intent to enjoy swimming and just work as hard as I could, get an education when I went to college, and find something I enjoyed.

My father helped me keep moving forward. We used to sit down before meets and set goals for me. If his time was faster, we'd compromise, and vice versa, if the time I wrote down was faster. That taught me how to set goals and make it a progression and was critical to my early motivation and success.

My little sister, parents, grandparents, aunts, and uncles all come to many of my meets. That support has been a big part of my success; without it my goals would not be possible.

In high school, I wasn't doing anything at the national level. I was happy doing things at the state level. To move up I knew I needed to put in a lot more work. But I had the desire—I wanted to do it.

I enjoy swimming against people who are better than I. That's always a reason to get up in the morning and work out hard, because I know there are swimmers out there getting better every day.

The No. 1 priority to me is having fun. If I'm not having a good time, it's not worth it. I always want to make sure in workouts or at swim meets that I'm having fun. If it gets to the point that I am not, I will have to sit down and re-evaluate things.

When I was a senior in high school, I narrowed my choices of colleges to the University of Arizona and Southern Cal. I chose USC because I wanted to go into communications, and I thought its communications program was better. So my college choice was based on education. At that time, I have to admit I didn't know that I would be able to accomplish what I've done in college.

I did what I was told in college. I never expected to be swimming the 200-meter backstroke and the 500-meter freestyle. My coach, Mark Schubert, and assistant coach Larry Lebowitz thought I should swim the 500 free and 200 back at the Pac-10 meet. "See what you can do," my coach said.

That ended up being a big turning point. If I had known that I'd be doing longer distances in college, I might have focused on that in high school.

So after winning conference in the 500 free, I went to the NCAA meet. I was overwhelmed, nervous, and didn't know what to expect. Teammate Kristine Quance asked me, "Are you OK?" Here I was, a freshman, and I was seeded No. 1 in the event at the NCAA Championships. Looking back, having great teammates was key to pushing me to improve and keeping me motivated and focused. It takes a lot of building blocks in place to form a successful project, and I've been in a position to have that throughout my career. The importance of that can't be overstated.

I set goals for workouts, not just for meets. That's the only way to get through the training hours. It's not an easy job going day by day. I try to enjoy it as much as I can, but it's not always a piece of cake. I have to remember I am training every set for a reason and to get better down the road. I sing songs in the pool at workouts. That helps me get through it, making it fun.

The trials for the 1998 world championships in 1997 were the summer between my junior and senior years. I did well in the 200 free and got second place, which put me on the relay and individual event at the world championships. I remember having dinner with my parents after the trials, and we talked about how I was taking things one step at a time. There is no way to make a huge gain in a short time span in swimming. It takes time and I had to keep the big picture in focus.

I didn't change a thing with what I was doing. Things seemed to fall into place.

I kept my focus in the classroom, too. I always believed that school came first. If I don't have an education, I won't be able to do anything. Our coach at USC, Mark Schubert, is really good about that. He'll let us miss a workout or make up our workout schedule if we need any extra time for school.

Also, I've kept my priorities in place. I know the key for me is time management. After the NCAAs each year when I have a break, I don't know how I'm able to manage swimming and school. Yet I actually do better when I'm busier. During that week off, I really don't do as well with my time management. But that's part of the beauty of having a break, getting my batteries recharged and maybe stepping my schedule back for a week to keep my focus.

Even though swimming is a big part of my life, I have to keep a balance or I will go crazy. The people who live swimming—eat, breathe and sleep it—will struggle at some point because they won't have fun at it. Everything can revolve around swimming if the person allows it. But having other interests balances life and makes that far less likely to happen.

Certainly, some people will always think of me as a swimmer, or know me because of what I did as a swimmer. But that is not who I am as a person. It's not something I tell.

That said, swimming has been very good for me. It's taught me dedication, perseverance, and determination. I've learned to work with people and be part of a team through swimming—something I couldn't learn from a job at this age. The traveling aspect has been awesome. I went to Europe in the summer of 1999 and that was a blast. I love to go to other cultures and learn about them. I respect them as I expect others to respect our country when they are here. But those cultures provide such a good learning experience.

So who knows where I'd be without swimming. I get so much enjoyment and pleasure from it. Young swimmers have to understand that success at the highest level doesn't happen overnight. It can't be expected to just happen. Any success comes from hard work and dedication. So if a young person isn't willing to do that, maybe this isn't the sport for him if his goal is to be an elite-level athlete. And that's not a bad thing. Swimming recreationally can do a lot for someone as well.

When I sign autographs, I write, "Follow your dreams," because dreams make anything possible.

When I was little, I wanted to go to the Olympics. I thought, "I can do it, no problem." But that's not reality, of course, because a child doesn't know any better. It wasn't until my junior year at USC that I realized this dream had even a chance of becoming true.

I will take what I've learned from swimming and apply it to life. I've had 16 years of dedicating myself to the physical and mental demands of swimming. I know that will help me later.

At this stage, obviously there are pressures. But I have to deal with them in my own way. I just do my best. If it goes well, that's great. If not, I'm still going to go back and work out the next day just as if I had won. So the idea is to give 100 percent, be happy with what you accomplished, learn and move forward.

Swimming has so much to offer. I'll stay in the sport as long as it's fun. If it's not fun, it's not worth it. It's important to set goals in life, but you also need to enjoy life as well.

JOHN ROETHLISBERGER
GYMNASTICS

Name: John Roethlisberger
Sport: Gymnastics
Born: June 21, 1970, Fort Atkinson, Wisconsin
Family: Wife, Kelly
Resides: Falcon Heights, Minnesota
Trains: University of Minnesota
Coaches: Fred Roethlisberger, Russ Fystrom, Thom Glielmi

Accomplishments: Two-time Olympian (1992, 1996); world championships team member (1994, 1995, 1997), 1990, 1992, 1993, 1995 national all-around champion; 1991 world championships team member (alternate); McDonald's American Cup titles in 1995 and 1996, the first male to do so since Peter Vidmar in 1983 and 1984; selected "Athlete of the Year" for 1990, 1992, 1993 and 1995 and co-winner in 1996 in voting by his national teammates; three-time NCAA all-around champion; four-time Big Ten all-around champion; 10 years on senior national team (1989-99); two years on junior national team (1987, 1989)

Hobbies: Golfing, video production, public/motivational speaking

Post-Olympic goals and plans: Would like to get more involved in public speaking and possibly even broadcasting. Would like to use my degrees in international business and finance to run my own business.

By John Roethlisberger

I've drawn a lot of strength and motivation from my family. My father, Fred, was on the 1968 U.S. men's olympic gymnastics team.

My sister, Marie, was a member of the 1984 U.S. Women's Olympic Gymnastics team. Many people thought there was added pressure on me to be a great gymnast, since my dad and sister were. That really wasn't the case. Having them pave the way gave me a big advantage—I learned from role models who were in my own home. Growing up, I wanted to go to the Olympics, but it wasn't until I was about 14 that I got serious about it.

In 1989, I made the U.S. senior national team, and I was just two spots away from making the U.S. world championship team.

In 1990, I won the U.S. national championship. That was an awesome experience because it came as somewhat of a surprise. If you'd have asked any coaches or athletes before the competition, not one of them would have picked me to win, and I wouldn't have been offended. I wasn't looked at as a contender yet and didn't think of myself as one.

In 1991, I came in as the defending national champion and was thus expected to make the U.S. world championship team. I had never been a favorite before and I didn't handle it well. I faltered and finished one spot away from making the team. It was a bad experience, but I learned how to handle being a frontrunner. In the long run it made me a better gymnast, especially with the 1992 Olympics on the horizon.

Fortunately, in 1992 I came back and won the national championship, which was a huge step toward making the 1992 Olympic team. I went on to make the '92 team and was looking forward to the greatest experience of my gymnastics career to that point. The 1992 Olympic Games were in Barcelona. Going into the Games I knew I was a good gymnast, but I wasn't quite at the level where I could be in the top ten or win a medal.

But the Olympics were still an incredible experience. I got out of it what the Olympics are supposed to be—competing in the front of the world, the excitement of being there, and taking part in the greatest sporting event. Even before the Olympics, I thought that, regardless of the results, I would learn from and enjoy my Olympic experience. It was also special because I had the opportunity to be on the Olympic stage with my dad as my coach. That is something that few fathers and sons will ever experience.

Up to that point, the 1992 Olympics were by far my biggest international competition. In a lot of ways, I was sort of thrust out there on the world stage. I didn't place really high on any event. I finished as the second-best American. I was 34th in the all-around and managed top-20 finishes in a couple of events. To see those numbers, it's not that great. But to me it was incredible—34th-best in the world after just entering the national scene, much less international. One thing that the 1992 Olympics really did for me was to fire me up to work harder, get better, and be a contender in the next Olympics.

I might not have the biggest, most impressive trick at a competition, but I will be clean and hit, and occasionally throw, something that may be surprising. I consider myself talented and am thankful for what God has given me. I don't look at my natural physical ability as an overwhelming asset, especially not compared to a lot of guys in the sport. I consider my strengths to be my perseverance and work ethic. It takes a long time for me to learn tricks and to get to the level where I need to be. So from the moment the 1992 Olympics ended, I knew I had to make every day and every moment count as I prepared for 1996.

There was a lot going on after the '92 Games. There were four world championships coming up before the '96 Games and I had a year of college gymnastics left. I wanted to win nationals again.

So, in that regard, college really helped. After the Olympics, some guys have a letdown. I was able to return to my team at the University of Minnesota and get fired up for another college season and try to win that elusive NCAA team championship. For me, being on the college team was as important as being on the Olympic team. I was part of a great university and a great tradition. It becomes a big part of you—it's like a family. To this day, the biggest regret I have is I wasn't able to bring home an NCAA team championship to the University of Minnesota.

I was definitely starting to feel more confident about what I could do internationally. In 1994 at the world championships I was 17th. I was second at the American Cup in 1994, so I was having good competitions. I was starting to make the climb and I needed to improve the difficulty of my optional routines to make the jump to the top ten.

As it turned out, 1995 was one of my best years. I won two gold and two silver medals at the Pan American Games. I also won my first American Cup and was fourth national all-around champion. I got to the point where I felt I could compete with the best in the world. My finishes in the compulsories, fifth in the world in 1995 and third in 1996, helped me build my confidence as a strong all-arounder.

This confidence seemed to flow over into my optionals and they started to improve. I thought my eighth place finish after the team competition at the 1995 world championships showed that. Unfortunately I went on to have very disappointing all-around finals, which meant my chance at the top ten would have to wait. Nonetheless, I felt that I had established myself as a strong all-arounder. One of the most important things I learned is that I might not be the best on paper or in some people's minds, but that didn't matter. The only thing that matters is what I do out on the floor, and in gymnastics that means anyone can excel.

At the 1996 Olympics in Atlanta, our team approached it differently than in 1992. In 1992 we were all wide-eyed and in awe of the entire Games. In 1996 we definitely had on our game faces. We wanted to go in there and hit every routine we did, and we trusted ourselves that we were good enough to win a medal as long as we took care of our business. We didn't care who was in the meet or how good they were. We were just concerned about our team. I ended up finishing seventh place in the all-around. That's not a medal, but being a contender for a medal is where I wanted to be—the goal was top ten.

The big feeling of disappointment was for the team. I wanted to medal, but, more importantly, I wanted the U.S. team to medal. I was heartbroken when we left the floor. I had never been so upset in my life. The U.S. men's program had struggled for so many years. I wanted to get respect for the U.S. men's team and I knew if we won a medal we'd have that respect. I thought, "Oh no, we didn't win a medal and thus we didn't win that respect." In some ways, getting respect from the gymnastics community and the fans is more important than winning a medal. As I look back now at how hard we battled and how much heart we put into our Olympic dream, I think we did get a great deal of respect.

To be frank, after the 1996 Olympics my father flat-out told me he wanted me to retire. He got upset when I said I wanted to train for the Games in 2000. "You've done enough," he told me, "you've had a great career. Retire!"

I talked to my fiancee—Kelly McConnell, a former gymnast who is now my wife—and I told her I wanted to continue. "I don't know why," I said, "but I just can't give this up. I have more in me. I want to keep going. I want to be a part of bringing an Olympic and world medal to the United States."

She understood, so I pushed forward.

In 1997, we went to the world championships. Going into the sixth event—the floor exercise—we were tied for third. We were awesome the entire competition. We had only one miss in the team finals out of all the routines. None of the other teams came close to hitting that percentage. The last event was floor, which I didn't do, but everyone competed unbelievably well. It was the best team performance on floor I had ever seen. We were going to do it, I thought—get top three and medal. Unfortunately, the other teams did higher-scoring routines, and we finished in fifth place. It was disappointing, but we had an awesome performance and were among the top five teams in the world, and that was success.

The 1998 season ended up being one of the toughest years ever for me. I started out with the Winter Cup and I had a terrible competition, finishing ninth. I went on to the American Cup and it was my worst ever, the first time I didn't make the all-around finals. I was trying to learn new stuff, and I couldn't hit my routines. I was struggling.

The improvement came slowly. At an intra-squad meet in June, I still didn't look polished, but I ended up in second place. Gradually, I improved at each meet. I knew it would pay off if I remained patient and kept plugging away without losing my confidence.

But August 20 at the U.S. national championships proved to be a bad day. Going into it, I thought all the struggling would pay off. I was in as good a shape as I'd been in my life. In practice I was nailing my routines.

The first event was the pommel horse. I had a new routine. I nailed it and won. I had a new ring routine, which I did well, and finished third. I went to the vault to warm up and felt good. Looking back I think I relaxed a little too much. I wasn't working the landing hard enough and I came in a little crooked and hurt my knee. When I landed I felt my knee shift out and back into the socket. It was an awful feeling. I thought my competition was over. I tried to shake it off by jogging and doing some standing backs. It felt OK but it was definitely unstable. All I could muster on vault was a handspring, but I couldn't quit.

I had worked so hard throughout the year and had come so far that I couldn't just walk away. I did the parallel bars and watered down the dismount because of the knee. I went to the high bar and even though I did a very easy dismount, my knee couldn't take it, and it popped out again. This time I knew I couldn't continue.

I had torn my anterior cruciate ligament completely, damaged the meniscus, and sprained the medial collateral ligament badly.

Now that I think about it, I should have stopped after the vault incident. The trainer checked it and there seemed to be something in the knee holding it together, at least until that high bar dismount. I am very stubborn. That quality has helped me reach some lofty goals, but in this case it kept me from seeing the big picture.

I underwent surgery and was on crutches for six weeks. However, I never doubted that I'd come back. In fact, I thought, "This will be awesome when I come back from this. There's no doubt I'll have the fastest recovery ever. I'll come back and be better than everyone could possibly imagine."

But it wasn't easy. The first week after the surgery was horrible. Once I got past the first week, I got back in the gym as soon as possible. I did anything I could—lifting weights or whatever. I made up exercises to get stronger. I used the injury as a motivational tool. It really fueled my desire to come back.

I knew it would have been easier to retire, but that wasn't an option. In February 1999 I went to Winter Cup. I didn't do the floor or vault, and in the other routines I didn't do dismounts. I just kind of used it to get back on the floor and to be a part of the U.S. team.

It's been a long road, and I don't know where it will end in terms of my goal of returning to the Olympics in 2000. But I know when I look back, I'll have no regrets, because I will know that I have put everything I have into reaching my goals, and I've done as much as I could with what I've been given.

I enjoy speaking to kids. I tell them to go after their dreams and not to let anyone stand in their way. But don't lie to yourself about what it will take to realize those dreams. It will take a lot of work, determination, and perseverance to reach any goal, especially those very lofty goals. I've lived by the motto that you "pack your lunch every day." It's not always glamorous and not always fun, but you have to work hard. If you do, the rewards will be worth every drop of sweat you've left in your trail.

BARB METZ LINDQUIST
TRIATHLON

Name: Barb Metz Lindquist
Sport: Triathlon
Born: July 1, 1969, Wilmington, Delaware
Family: Husband, Loren Lindquist; Brother, Albert; Sister-in-law Julie; Nephew, Jake; Mother, Kathy Metz; Father, Albert Metz
Resides: Jackson, Wyoming
Hometown: Casper, Wyoming
Coach: Loren Lindquist

Accomplishments: 1998 USOC Athlete of the Year; 1998 National City Bank Triathlon champion; 1998 USTS—Madison, Wisconsin; Champion; 1998 USTS—Oceanside, California, champion; 1998 Pao de Acucar Triathlon silver medalist; 1998 St. Croix (USVI) International Triathlon silver medalist; 1998, '97 Escape From Alcatraz Triathlon silver medalist; 1998 Goodwill Games fourth place, top American: 1997 National City Bank Triathlon silver medalist; 1997 ITU World Cup—Gamagori, Japan, bronze medalist; 1997 ITU World Cup—Sydney, Australia, bronze medalist; 1996 Sado Island Long Course Triathlon silver medalist; 1991 Pan American Games 200-meter free and 400-meter free silver medalist, 4x200-meters free relay gold medalist; 1989 Pan Pacific 1,500-meter freestyle silver medalist; 1989 Alamo Cup 800-meter freestyle bronze medalist; 1987 Pan American Games 400-meter freestyle silver medalist; 1986 U.S. Open 200-meter freestyle bronze medalist

Hobbies: Reading, cross-country skiing, skate skiing, napping

Post-Olympic goals and plans: Coaching, running bed and breakfast training camps

By Barb Metz Lindquist

Swimming has always been a big part of my life. I started swimming when I was eight and swam through college until I was 21. In addition to being on the U.S. national team from 1987 to 1991, I competed in the U.S. Olympic Trials in 1988.

At the 1988 Trials, I had three great swims and was really happy with how I raced. But that was the Janet Evans era for distance swimmers, so there was really only one spot open since Janet was in a league of her own. I made the finals in three events and took sixth, seventh, and eighth places. I thought my chances of representing the U.S. in the Olympics were over when I retired from swimming in 1991. Little did I know that more than a decade later I would have a second shot at the Olympic team, this time in triathlon.

I graduated from Stanford in 1991 and finished my last swim meet, the Pan American Games in Cuba, that same summer. I didn't quite know what I wanted to do with my life.

My family had built a house in Jackson, Wyoming, in 1980, which we used for summer vacations, Christmas holidays, and long weekends while I was growing up. After I graduated from college, my mom said, "You've swum hard and studied hard. Take a break and have some fun. Why don't you live in our house in Jackson, wait tables at night, and play all day?"

She told me I should "play in God's great playground," the nearby Grand Teton National Park. It didn't take much arm-twisting for me to take that deal. I thought I'd do that for a year and then find a job working for an environmental organization before heading to graduate school. I took a job waiting tables at night at our local Chinese food restaurant, and enjoyed the outdoors and sleeping in. One year of doing this soon turned into two and Mom started to wonder if she should have made the offer!

In January 1993, Jackson opened an indoor pool—the only ones to that point were at the hotels. The opportunity to coach the summer swim team opened up in 1993. The woman who started the program was pregnant with her fourth child and she was waiting for the right person to hand her "baby"—the swim team—to. I took over the program and, with the help of a great parents' board, turned it into a year-round operation with the opening of the indoor pool. Then I started a boys' and girls' high school team.

I had swum for great coaches over the years, both at the national level and growing up in Casper. Six-time Olympic coach George Haines coached me my first year at Stanford. Following him was Richard Quick, one of the current Olympic coaches. I picked the best of what I learned from both of these coaches, as well as from my best age group coaches, Gregg Waterman, Dave Hoch, Ed Spencer, Ralph Crocker, and Gary Butts. I drew from them everything from creative training sets, mental focusing techniques, dry land training, and coaching styles and used it to create my own coaching style in Jackson.

Coaching swimmers made me a better swimmer. I had to learn how to explain things. When I was swimming, all I had to do was listen and do it. As a coach, when you explain technique, it clarifies things in your own mind as to why you do certain drills, and why you do those a certain way.

I coached in the late afternoons and waited tables at night. Basically, I was still free my whole day to play outside. The first two things I bought were studded snow tires for my car and a pedal and shoe system for my old college bike.

I spent the days bike riding and doing trail running in Grand Teton National Park. Even though I enjoyed the freedom of doing whatever I wanted when I woke up, I longed for a bit of structure. After putting on some weight I felt I needed a challenge and goal, so I decided to do a triathlon with a friend. I did the 1993 Spudman Triathlon in Burley, Idaho, about three hours away.

My strength would obviously be the swim. But the Spudman swim was downstream in the Snake River, and the currents and conditions pretty much nullified any advantage I thought I had. I swam the mile in ten minutes, six minutes faster than I did in my peak of swimming in a pool. You have to love that current!

It was a fun race. It was a perfect first event because the local Lions Club was superb in organizing it. I found that the other triathletes were a unique group: fun loving, helpful, and very healthy. I came in third place. I wasn't thinking about turning pro or anything, but I did think, "Hey, this is fun. I'm learning a lot." It also encouraged me to continue.

Two years later I joined our local cycling club's Tuesday night ride and I met Loren, who would become my husband. He helped me with my cycling technique. For one thing, he told me my seat was too high. Later I teased him and asked him what he was doing looking at my seat! A few days after that ride I asked him if he would be my support crew at a triathlon I was doing that weekend in Vernal, Utah. He agreed, so we drove five hours to the race, talking and getting to know each other along the way.

At the race he saw this potential for me to take the triathlon to the elite level, and also the potential for me to be his wife. Not necessarily in that order! Two months later he proposed and six months after that we were married in April 1996. On our honeymoon the next weekend I did my first two professional races at St. Anthony's and St. Croix. My calves were still sore at the races from dancing at our wedding reception in heels the week before.

I did six races in 1996, while still coaching, to see if I had the potential to do well and to see if I enjoyed it. Quite frankly, I had done the amateur sport thing for so long with swimming, that I didn't have a huge desire to do triathlon unless I could make a living at it. After that first season we thought I had that potential. I gave up coaching in the spring of 1997 to become a full-time triathlete.

A lot of people were surprised by how quickly I improved. I credit much of that to my swimming background. Some people think swimming is really boring, going back and forth in a pool, staring at a black line. There's not much visual stimulation, so you have to keep yourself entertained mentally. In college when I'd swim for hours I'd write the introductory paragraph for a term paper, translate songs into French, pray through my prayer list, or concentrate on technique. Cycling and running have been easy to adapt to because there are so many beautiful things to look at.

As a swimmer, I have to pay attention to technique and do a lot of drills. I do a lot of fine-tuning and playing with my stroke. Because of this, I've been open to doing drills on the bike and run. There is more technique involved in riding a bike than the average person would think. Since I have the mentality of a distance swimmer, I'm not afraid of the pain or monotony of training a lot. I've also been fortunate in regard to injuries. If I have a nagging injury here or there, I realize the importance of backing off for a while and taking it easy. My husband has been good at monitoring this. I know it's better to take a day off now, rather than a week off later by aggravating the injury and not letting it heal.

I do enjoy the swim. I feel so comfortable in the water and it makes me so relaxed. It's a feeling I liken to being back in my mother's womb. Having my best event first in the triathlon puts me in a relaxed place mentally starting each race.

I do have a good focus and perspective in my life. I am a Christian. My No. 1 priority in my life is my relationship with God. Number two is my relationship with Loren. Number three is triathlon. So I've told God, "If ever two and three get in front of one, whack me upside the head until I get my priorities back in line."

When I was swimming I had my identity all wrapped up in being a swimmer. If I had a good swim I felt like a great person, but if I had a bad swim, I felt lousy about myself. My self-worth was related to how I did at the meets. Eventually in the last year of swimming competitively, I was swimming out of fear. When I got on the blocks I was so afraid of failing that I dreaded racing. Now as a Christian my attitude is totally different. My identity is wrapped up in Christ. I know that God loves me regardless of how I perform out there on the course. His love is unconditional. I don't need to get my self worth from what I do. God proved how worthy I am to him by sending Jesus to die for me. Now when I line up for a race, I am excited, not fearful, for what God will do through me on that day. It is 180-degree difference in how I view racing, from fearful to fun.

I feel like the triathlon is my mission field. Some missionaries travel to Africa or Central America to spread God's word. Well, in the triathlon, the worlds come to the races. There are people from all countries and backgrounds. I feel that God wants to use me in these races to be a "light" in a dark world. He can do that in both good and bad race results, and he has (though I prefer when he uses me in the good races!)

I feel like God has given me these talents. It's my desire to glorify Him. If I cave in or don't give 100 percent, I'm feel like I am cheating God because he's given me these talents. I don't feel like I'm doing these talents justice.

I still have plenty of room for improvement. The successes I have experienced have been great. But I can still get a lot better on the bike and run, and even the swim.

I was blessed to win a stage in the beginning of 1999 at the Formula One Triathlon in Australia, something no non-Australian woman had ever done. But one race does not a champion make. That one race is just a stepping stone to where I want to go. I don't get all wrapped up in a win or high placing. I won't get complacent. Other people have been more excited about my placings or wins than I have. There are a lot of other great triathletes in the U.S., not to mention in the world.

Training and competing are still fun for me. I wouldn't do it if it weren't. My husband wants to make sure I enjoy it. We get to travel, see some beautiful parts of the world, and make some lifelong friends. With all these races I feel like I am on a reconnaissance mission to stake out places we'd like to return to for a vacation. I imagine a vacation where I just have to pack one small bag and not all the swim, bike, and run gear that go into a huge bike box!

VITALY MARINITCH
GYMNASTICS COACH

Name: Vitaly Marinitch
Sport: Gymnastics Coach
Born: Nov. 23, 1970, Odessa, Ukraine
Family: Wife, Olga; daughter, Lilia
Resides: Colorado Springs, Colorado
Hometown: Colorado Springs, Colorado
Coaches at: Olympic Training Center

Accomplishments: American Cup all-around champion and four individual events winner in 1989; member of gold medal world champion team and bronze medalist on still rings in Germany, 1989; bronze medalist on pommel horse at the 1994 world championships in Brisbane, Australia; member of bronze medalist team at 1994 world championships in Germany; gold medalist in vaulting, and still rings silver medalist at 1991 Professional World Championships

Hobbies: Spending time with my daughter Lilia, golf, skiing, tennis, computers

Post-Olympic goals and plans: Don't know yet

By Vitaly Marinitch

I grew up in Odessa, Ukraine, where there weren't enough goods for living. A person could not afford many good things. Salaries were not high enough to afford a car. Vehicles could not be leased or financed, so it took ten years to save enough to buy one, and even then, you'd have to settle for a car that wasn't very good.

Of course, I was in the Soviet army. I had to be. My heart wasn't in it, but my sports division wasn't really the Red Army, although we were considered army. I had all the uniforms, but my mission was sports, and since there was a big focus on sports, they let us do our thing.

The uncertainty of the fall of the Soviet Union was exciting and scary. Nobody knew what would happen next. The exciting part was moving toward capitalism. People had a chance to run their own businesses.

When the Soviet Union collapsed and the various states broke into independent countries, the situation was worse for a while. Everyone was separated because of the breakup and the lack of continuity hurt the businesses. If one company made a car in one state, it needed different parts from other states, which had become different countries. Even with cars it presented big logistical problems. One republic had the tires, another had engines and they couldn't put the car together. They had to start all over. Moscow got all the embassies so that was good for them. But every other republic had to build embassies. So it was tough.

I knew life wasn't as good as it was in other places, particularly the United States. What did I like about the U.S.? I knew it was a good life, or at least a better life than I had in Ukraine.

I stopped competing as a gymnast in Ukraine in late 1994. I was issued a visa to be in the United States. USA Gymnastics worked on my visa to help me leave. The head gymnastics coach of Ukraine wasn't very happy. I left the team as we were preparing for the 1996 Olympics. I could have helped that team in the Olympics. At that time I got a great opportunity to come to the U.S. and work at the Olympic Training Center. So my wife and I came to America in January 1995.

It's harder to leave Ukraine now. I'm trying to get my parents over here to visit, but the U.S. Embassy will not issue visas for them because they are afraid my parents would stay here for good. It's upsetting.

Getting accustomed to the U.S. wasn't a problem for me—I got used to it pretty quickly. When I first came here, everything was hugely different. Going to the store was the biggest change, seeing stuff on the shelves everywhere. There were no crowds, no lines of people fighting and cursing, trying to get things.

It is easy to get food here. When I was in Ukraine it was really difficult to get good food in the stores. The only place was at the flea markets, and that was expensive. You could live well there, but it was costly.

Going to the malls here was a shock. My eyes and mouth were wide open in awe. I had traveled through my career as a gymnast, so I knew about the things that capitalism could provide. I thought, "Wow, I can't believe how well people in this kind of system can live!"

Now I know that I made the right decision to move to America, although I always wonder what would have happened had I stayed in Ukraine. I don't know what I would have done. But I did know I had an uncertain future and no money. It was constantly a struggle—a hard life.

I started coaching when I came to America. I had some friends here and I asked them to find me a job. They called the U.S. Gymnastics Federation. Ron Brant, the resident coach at the Olympic Training Center in Colorado Springs, was looking for a coach to join him at that time.

I took the job and enjoyed coaching right away.

I was very excited about my job. I worked with several gymnasts then. One of them was John Macready. Because Coach Brant wanted what was best for the team, he let me go as John's coach to the 1996 Olympic Games. Ron more than deserved to go, but he wanted what was best for the team. Since I had worked closely with John for the 18 months prior to the Olympics, Ron determined that I was a better choice to go. That was very generous on Coach Brant's part.

Here I was, in the U.S. for just over a year and I was able to represent the U.S. at the Olympics in 1996 as a coach. I could never have envisioned that when I was leaving Ukraine. Going to the Olympics was a great experience. It's hard to describe what I felt at the 1996 Games. It was interesting because I had a wide array of emotions. I was kind of jealous of the Ukraine team, because I could have been with them as a competitor, and at the same time I was proud that I was John's coach, too, representing America. As I look back, leaving Ukraine when I did was a big step. I had a choice to compete in the Olympics or move to the United States. I chose the U.S. to start a new life.

My daughter has more opportunities here. The education and lifestyle here give her chances she would not have had in the Ukraine. I am so grateful for that. I can appreciate it and so can my wife.

We've been everywhere in Colorado. We ski in the mountains and really enjoy the scenery. I don't think I'll ever go back to Ukraine for good. I will go to visit. My parents haven't seen their granddaughter. I am trying to get them here, but it is tough.

America is a different country in other ways. The people have a life that is almost too good, but I don't think they appreciate what they have. There are a lot of people who are really lazy and don't want to work hard. They'd rather complain. The young people of America face a challenge of not getting lazy from being spoiled. In that regard, it helped me to grow up in Ukraine because I learned lessons I would not have learned here.

I'm still not that patriotic, just because I came over when I was already an adult. But my daughter is an American and I'm sure she'll have a bigger feeling of pride from being born here.

MARK RUIZ
DIVING

Name: Mark Ruiz
Sport: Diving
Born: April 9, 1979, Rio Piedra, Puerto Rico
Family: Mother, Lydia Torres; Father: John Ruiz;
Stepfather, Armando Velez; Brother, John Ruiz; Sister, Giselle Ruiz
Resides: Orlando, Florida
Hometown: Toa Alta, Puerto Rico
Trains: YMCA Aquatic Center in Orlando, Florida
Coach: Jay Lerew

Accomplishments: 13-time national champion; 1998 Diver of the Year (first male to do that since Greg Louganis in 1988); 1999 Pan-American Games 3-meter gold medalist
Hobbies: Golf, basketball
Post-diving goals and plans: Business owner

By Mark Ruiz

I was taking swimming lessons at age four in Puerto Rico when I saw some kids diving off the board.

I wanted to dive, though I did it just for fun at the time.

When I was nine, I took swimming lessons at the University of Puerto Rico. The coach saw me dive and said I had some talent and he talked to my mom. She had her own business to run and was very busy.

"What time is diving practice?" my mom asked.

"For his age group, it's at 2 p.m.," the coach, Hector Bass, said.

"I can't do that," my mom said. "I have too many commitments."

The coach suggested I dive with the senior group since I could be at practice at that time without interfering with my mom's schedule. None of the parents of the seniors were happy. But I learned and worked really hard. Six months later, as a ten-year-old, I made the Puerto Rico national team for the Central American Games.

To tell you the truth, the parents didn't want me on the team. But I beat the two kids whose parents thought they were better than I was. I did pretty well at the Central American Games, which are held every two years.

I was 12 years old and improving quickly. After winning the Central American Games, my coach asked for a raise because he had been doing such a good job. He didn't get the raise and resigned from the team to make a better living.

"Mark," Hector said. "I want you to go to a training camp in Orlando."

I wasn't a good fit with the coach who replaced him. He was the kind who yelled and was pretty rough. I went to Orlando and had the best time of my life. I was so happy. I had never seen a pool so nice.

The coach for the Orlando team, Jeff Schafer, really liked the way I dived. He thought I had talent so he asked me if I wanted to move to Florida. I talked to Hector.

"That's the best decision you can make," Hector said. "You'll do a lot better. Over here you won't make it as far, even if I stayed as your coach. The U.S. program knows a lot more about diving. It's a great opportunity to get better."

My mother had her business, but she wanted to give me this great chance. She sold her business and we moved to Orlando, just the two of us. To this day I can't believe how awesome that was of her, to move here and give up everything for me.

I started diving with Jeff. I kept getting better and better, but I couldn't compete for the U.S. for two years since I had competed for Puerto Rico. So when I was 14 I went to my first junior nationals in Pasadena, California, where the kids had heard about me. I had a good meet winning the three-meter and platform and taking second on the one-meter. From there on I kept improving.

Jeff took a job as coach at Louisiana State University and resigned from Team Orlando. He had taught me a lot.

The new coach, KZ Li, was from China. Of course I was nervous having a new coach. But KZ was great. He taught me more mechanics and how to dive from the 10-meter. Really, when I started off from the 10-meter, it was really easy for me to do the dives.

From there I kept getting better and better. I started growing when I was 16. I was about 5 feet tall and all of the sudden I was 5-foot-7. My bones and tendons weren't developing as fast, and my wrists hurt a lot. Some days it was so bad I couldn't even dive off of one meter.

I dived fairly well in the Olympic Trials in April 1996, although I had struggled before that. At the Trials I wasn't nervous. My attitude was, "Hey, I have nothing to lose. I will learn from this."

I did better in finals than in prelims. In this level of competition, both prelim and finals scores count. If I had done as well in prelims I would have been a top four or so and been in contention for the Olympic Team. But I missed one or two dives in the prelims.

That taught me a lot, but afterward I was drained and still hurting. I took about a month off, started training for junior nationals, and won the platform. I was still growing, but I was starting to get some strength in my wrists.

In 1997, I was second at senior nationals on platform. Right after that, KZ left to coach at the University of Minnesota. Jay Lerew was our new coach. I wasn't sure I wanted to train with him, but I heard he was a very good coach. Plus, I loved Orlando and diving, and Jay knew I had a love for the sport.

Again, it was like the other coaching change. With Jeff, I learned a basic foundation, and KZ came in and helped me to another level with different skills. KZ and I had some communication problems from time to time in the pool but otherwise we got along great. I thank him for what he did for me on the platform. But Jay took me from there and it was just great. I had been so serious.

"Play around and have fun and enjoy diving again," Jay said. He took it easy on me for the next year or so.

A big turning point came for me in Austria in July 1997. I beat Dmitri Sautin, and no American had beaten him since 1992, when Mark Lenzi beat him in the Olympics. I thought, "I can't believe I beat Dmitri." I did really well to keep up with him. I had to follow him in the finals since I had beaten him in the previous round. Never had I followed such a great diver. I learned that when I follow such a great diver I have to have the presence and peace of mind to follow with a great dive.

It was a great experience because from then on I had the confidence that I knew I could beat anybody. If I could beat Dmitri once, I could beat anybody. Jay noticed it and he started pushing me to train hard.

At the World Trials in 1997, I was able to experience the same kind of meet as the Olympic Trials. I put in the time and really started training hard. At the World Trials I won the platform. I was so far ahead I didn't even have to do my last dive and I still could make the world championship team. I took sixth place at the world championships. I wasn't too happy with it because I wanted to get a medal for the United States.

In the summer of 1998, I won the three-meter, platform, and synchronized platform at senior nationals. At the outdoor nationals in August 1998, I won tower, for three national titles.

My coach and I were happy, but he knew I could do better. I didn't do my best on three-meter.

I kept improving. From the outdoor nationals in August 1998, I made the World Cup team and went to New Zealand where I took third place on platform, just a point out of second place and was the only U.S. individual medalist.

In April 1999, the indoor nationals were in Orlando. I was in my own pool with the home crowd. I won one-meter. I missed my first dive on three-meter, so I didn't start out well. From there I got more consistent and picked up high scores. I was behind by 20 points going into my last dive. I got 9s and 9.5s, which got me to the top and I won. I dived fairly well on platform winning my ninth national title. I also won the men's all-around award for the whole meet.

My goal is the Olympics. I take great pride in representing the United States, which I have wanted to do since I was a little kid. It's been a dream to go to these big meets. I'm just fortunate. Regardless of where we compete, I want to do well for the U.S. If I can't do my best, I want someone else to go because the United States deserves the best.

The United States is my home country. I have grown up here and my friends and family live here. I have to take great pride in this country. Some people go to big meets and say, "What the heck? It's just a meet, I hope we do well, but if we don't, oh well." That's not the way I look at it. My main goal is to put the United States right back at the top of the world in diving.

Even though I was born in Puerto Rico and am an American citizen, moving to America was the most important thing we've done in our lives. That was a great thing. My mom sacrificed so much for me. I thank God for everything. While I've done well in diving, I'm more grateful for my family and the friends I have around me.

Diving has taught me so much. I now know that if I put my mind to it and keep working I can do well at it and I will improve. I've learned so much about being responsible, getting to practice on time, and dealing with expectations. I have been successful because I have such a great family and friends.

I love talking to kids. I tell them to do the best they can and not let anyone else put them down. I tell them to practice hard, but to have fun. But if it's not fun, it doesn't matter how good you are. If you are having fun, it's the greatest thing. That's why I do what I do. Even if I was good but I wasn't having fun, trust me, I wouldn't be doing it.

ROBIN GOAD
WEIGHTLIFTING

Name: Robin Goad
Sport: Weightlifting
Born: Jan. 1, 1970, Columbus, Georgia
Family: Husband, Dean Goad; Daughter, Sydney
Hometown: Newnan, Georgia
Resides: Newnan, Georgia
Trains: Private gyms
Coach: John Coffee and Ben Green

Accomplishments: 1994 world champion; 20 world championship medals, 10-time national champion, American (current) and world record holder (1991, 1994); the most decorated female weightlifter in the history of the sport; Pan Am gold medal winner

Hobbies: Raising my daughter, quilting, and shopping for antiques

Post-Olympic goals and plans: To expand my business, Kid Fit Gymnastics, and begin teaching weightlifting to young girls and boys

By Robin Goad

As a very young girl, I could shimmy up any tree, jump any fence, and carry around any items, like cinder blocks, that I happened to pick up. I never thought that one of these skills would someday take me to the Olympics, but I am counting on that now.

I was always athletic and I wanted an outlet to showcase my skills. I chose gymnastics because it seemed most natural to me. I was the little girl who was swinging from tree to tree, turning flips down the hill, and walking logs along our pond. I watched Nadia Comaneci win gold medals in the 1976 Olympics and I had my dream to one day compete in the Olympics. While I was still competing in gymnastics, my coach instructed me on how to do the snatch and clean and jerk lifts. He said they would help increase my strength and so I did it.

Meanwhile, this coach bragged about my strength to a weightlifting coach from Atlanta and hence my lifting career began at the age of 12.

When I started lifting weights in 1982, weightlifting as a sport for women was fairly uncharted waters, especially for younger girls. My teammates from Atlanta have since admitted that in the beginning I was the laughingstock of the team. Not because I wasn't strong but because I was a homecoming queen, cheerleader chick who, it was reasoned, would surely fold under pressure and never have the toughness to stick it out. Well, my story is just the opposite. Eighteen years later I am still proving them wrong and sticking it out.

I continued both sports for a couple of years, but finally came to the realization that I was a better weightlifter than gymnast and I had new goals to reach. While I enjoyed lifting, I also wanted to prove that women could lift weights and maintain their feminine side. So often female lifters are cast as freakish, like circus acts. Every time I am introduced as a weightlifter someone says, "You don't look like a weightlifter." And I always reply, "Yes, this is exactly what a weightlifter looks like. Take a good look and remember."

The other goal meant focusing on weightlifting and pushing the sport to a new level of international competition and Olympic inclusion. My then and current coach, John Coffee, who coached lifters who long dominated the national scene, knew how to press my buttons and pushed my athletic performance to where no other American woman had gone before. He's well respected and well known. I was fortunate to have lived near this brilliant coach who has molded and shaped my career.

My first goal to become a champion weightlifter was coming

true, but an even bigger battle was ahead, one that I had less control over. That was recognition of women's weightlifting as a sport. The first women's world championship was hosted by the USA in Daytona, Florida, in 1987. I was a part of that event and made sure that I have been a part of the rise of women's weightlifting on and off the platform ever since. At the 1999 Pan Am Games, over a decade later, I was walking history for my sport. I was determined to perform my best, lifting in the 116-pound class. I was successful at lifting a 187 lb. snatch and 225 lb. clean and jerk for a total of 412 pounds.

Competing in the Pan Am Games and knowing we would be an Olympic sport in 2000 was ever so sweet for me, but it also created some feelings of sadness. I had many close friends who helped to make this sport what it is today, and most of these women were either too old or too injured to qualify for these two meets. As lifters, we waited so long to have the opportunity to compete in these events that I felt they all had a right to be there with me. I felt so strongly about this that I sent all of them notes thanking them for the road they paved for those of us who made it. I also make sure new lifters are aware of our history. I feel like I represent weightlifters of the past and present. I am the woman who must bridge the gap between the pre-Olympic and post-Olympic athletes of this sport.

I feel fortunate to be where I am at this point. I've worked hard, and so did my friends from the past. I know my former teammates could appreciate this new journey on a whole different level just because of their perspective—not better or worse than the current team, just different. The pre-Olympic years were not bad; they were a learning process and a journey.

We spent many training hours and dedicated ourselves to a sport that withheld the financial support and resources that accompany most Olympic sports.

I went to the University of West Georgia so I could stay close to home and to my weightlifting coach. I worked hard in school, balancing an hour commute to the gym, a late night job, and school exams. The harder I work, the more I appreciate the rewards. I graduated at the top of my class, receiving honors, and earned my bachelor of science degree.

After college, I taught physical education and always tried to share my competition and travel experiences with my students. After winning the 1994 world championships I took the opportunity to give each of my students two souvenirs. One was a glass good luck eye from Turkey and the other was hope. Through me these children were able to witness a dream coming true that was won with hard work and determination.

After women's weightlifting was excluded from the 1996 Olympics in Atlanta, and we as yet had no word that they would be added to Sydney in 2000, I pretty much put weightlifting on the back burner. Inclusion in the Atlanta Olympics would have meant that I could have gone for the gold in front of family and friends in my home state. All the letters we sent to the media and officials pleading our case seemed to have made no impact.

We knew that adding our sport would take very little money, as all the equipment and venue arrangements were there for the men, and we just needed the room and board space. We'd have packed sack lunches and lived in our cars if we had had the chance to be in the Olympics. Instead of competing, I was just another spectator watching male weightlifters having medals draped around their necks, standing at attention for their national anthem. I was disappointed and heartbroken. I felt that I would never see the chance to make an Olympic team and I had to accept that and move on.

Dean and I were married in 1994 and we decided in 1996 after the Olympics that it was time to start our family. We were going to move on with our lives. We both felt we had seen the last hope for our Olympic participation pass by. I kept training, but it was no longer the most important thing in my life.

In March 1997, we had our baby girl. Her name is Sydney, the same name as the city in Australia hosting the 2000 Games. It makes a great story to say we named her in honor of the 2000 Games, only that's not true.

We named her Sydney just because we liked the name. Ironically, just a few days later we learned women's weightlifting was added for 2000. While people assume, even people close to us, that we named our little girl after the 2000 Games host city, it is purely coincidence. And we will certainly enjoy that.

Having women's weightlifting added to the Games is the opportunity for which we've waited. The support from USA Weightlifting and the USOC has been great. As a wife and mother of a toddler, I benefit greatly from the financial aid that enables me to stay at home and train hard. I never would have been able to balance working full time, training full time, and raising my daughter.

I was worried about getting back into training knowing that I had a child to take care of. I knew how time-consuming training at a high level was. At the time, I had not qualified for any stipend from the USOC or USA weightlifting. In the summer of 1997, I was forced to make a decision, to go back to work as a teacher or take a chance to try to make the team and qualify for assistance. Everything happened the right way, at the right time. I starting receiving my stipend, and the Olympic flame within me was re-ignited and burning brightly.

I've been on track in this comeback and positioned myself for a legitimate shot at the Olympic Games in 2000. This journey has shown me that I've succeeded on a level that is more than just personal. It is the sport itself that I love. Weightlifting gives me an avenue to build not only my physical attributes but also moral character.

Hopefully, when my run is over, I can help coach the women's weightlifting team, and by then I hope we'll have a full team represented at the Olympic Games.

Competing at this level is a valuable experience. I work and work and work, but I am still vulnerable when I step up on the platform to lift. I can win or even fail in front of millions of people, but the achievement of simply getting there is what shapes character, and I will take that with me the rest of my life. People say the weightlifting platform is the loneliest place in the world, but it taught me to believe in myself. I see nothing but a platform and a barbell. But there's so much more than that; people have spent years and years setting themselves up for that one moment in time. It can be tremendous pressure, pressure that many talented athletes fold under, but it can also be the best lesson in determination and spirit that one might ever face.

This sport has molded my life. Through the years when I got money for breaking records, I paid my way through school or paid bills. I broke my own records, got another check, and used that money wisely. I drew a tangible sustenance from the sport, as well as appreciating what it did for me mentally and physically.

I also met my husband Dean, an accomplished lifter who set numerous junior records and won medals in the Pan Am Games. How has this sport changed my life? Well, it's been my life. I don't know of a part of my life that hasn't been touched by this sport.

As a woman, this experience has taught me about the world and a woman's role in it. From the U.S. to Indonesia, India, and Europe, I know how to balance the soft nurturing side of being a female with the strong, educated, and athletic side. It is possible. There was a time when I was almost angry that there was an inequity in sports for women in general. But now, I see it from a different standpoint. Demanding equality with words feels different than demanding it with performance. We had to, and still have to, educate people about where women's weightlifting has been, where it is, and where we can take it.

It's just amazing what willpower can do. I don't want to give up. My journey is not over. The Olympics will be the light at the end of this long tunnel. I'm not there yet so I keep going.

Traveling these past few years has shown me so much about the great character of the women in the USA Weightlifting program. We represent so many faces of America—housewives, students, teachers and professionals of all ethnic races.

I love the team that I serve with now. Not one of us takes even a moment for granted. I've seen cocky jocks, and we don't have any on this team. No one accepts that anything will come easily. That's just not a possibility with this group. We've worked hard to get here, and we have a lot of hard work left. I draw a lot of inspiration from my teammates.

As a mother, I wonder if I'm doing enough for my daughter. All mothers I talk to wonder about that, regardless of their career. Part of me realizes I've given a majority of my life to weightlifting. When the 2000 Games are over, life will be fun and games. I might continue lifting, but if it takes away from being a mother and a wife, lifting will be put on the back burner.

But I will always have the skills and memories from lifting. Feeling strong carries over into other sports and into my overall persona. If I am physically fit and strong it shows in my appearance and how I carry myself. It translates into an internal strength, especially for young girls. It gives them confidence. I hope a lot of girls will see that.

ALLISON WESTON
VOLLEYBALL

Name: Allison Weston
Sport: Volleyball
Born: Feb. 19, 1974, Goldsboro, North Carolina
Family: Parents, Thomas and Diana; Brother, Michael
Hometown: Omaha, Nebraska
Resides: Colorado Springs, Colorado
Trains: Olympic Training Center
Coach: Mick Haley

Accomplishments: 1998 U.S. national team, coaches and players MVP Award winner. 1997: In second game as U.S. team member, posted 28 kills and two aces vs. Canada. College: Led Nebraska to 63-2 record in final two years, including 1995 NCAA Championship; 1995 All-American, first team, Conference Player of the Year, Academic All-American, NCAA All-Tournament first team

Hobbies: Fishing, hiking, anything outdoors

Post-Olympic goals and plans: Pursue a career in the field of natural resources

By Allison Weston

Sports have always been a big and very special part of my life.

I was kind of a late comer to volleyball in that I was in eighth grade when the junior high volleyball coach asked me to come out for the team.

My first and favorite sport was basketball at that point, but I wanted to be involved in something else since the season was only part of the year.

At the junior high level, volleyball is an ugly version of the real game. I stuck with it, though, and in high school the sport began to resemble the way it should be played.

I was still thinking about basketball at that point for college. But back then, there was no professional basketball league. I thought I had a better chance at reaching a higher level in volleyball, so I chose that.

I accepted a scholarship to the University of Nebraska at Lincoln. As a native of the Omaha area, going to the state's biggest university was important to me.

But when I showed up at the university, it took a couple of weeks to get into it and feel like I could play at that level. I was one of two freshmen. The coach, Terry Pettit, just threw us in there and said, "Do the best you can. Learn as you go." That was intimidating at first because there were some incredible athletes on the team, especially a few seniors. I took a couple of shots to the head in practice and that woke me up a bit.

We were able to achieve (win) the University of Nebraska's first national championship in volleyball in 1995, which was part of a 63-2 record over my final two years as a Husker. I have to attribute that to Coach Pettit. He kept people focused on the task at hand. That's my style, too; once I step on the court, it's time to get down to business and get the job done. I had a lot of great teammates who helped keep everyone focused.

A player has to understand that losing is just part of sports, and life. We can't always be on top every time we go out there. It's not the end of the world to lose a match or play badly. We can take the steps we need to achieve the success we are striving for and always be aware that we can get better.

In fact, I believe a lot more can be learned from a loss than from beating a team badly. That's what happened to us in 1995 at Nebraska.

We lost to Stanford at home in Lincoln early in the season. Nebraska had not won a national championship in volleyball, and Stanford had such a great tradition. We had opportunities to win that match but didn't. That showed us we needed to step it up and get after it. We learned so much from that match, and it ended up being our last loss of the year. It made us realize how hungry we truly were. That loss hurt so much. We finished the year realizing that if we wanted to be the best, we had to constantly work hard and stay focused.

The national championship was an incredible experience. Coach Pettit said it best: "This is something that will stick with you the rest of your life."

It definitely has. To go 63-2 over that span involved an incredible amount of focus and dedication. To set a goal that high and then achieve it, well, very few people can lay claim to such an accomplishment. It's a very rewarding experience. I learned a lot about myself, about teamwork, about goal setting and dedication. Really, it's just an amazing feeling to be the best in your category.

We hoped to lay the foundation for continued success at Nebraska. That is the legacy of a program: Reaching the top, and staying there without taking two steps back for every one step forward. I think I, along with the rest of the players, would be happy for any Nebraska team that bettered the run that we had. You set the bar at a certain level and others who follow push themselves harder to meet or exceed that standard.

To be a part of the U.S. national team now is something more than I ever expected. I'm excited that I can continue to play still at age 25.

At this level, it's a different kind of enjoyment. For kids, it is important to have fun and enjoy it. There are times they need to be intense and to remember what they are playing for. It's not fun all the time, but that's the case with anything. But in any sport, and at any level, enjoyment has to be found or there won't be a lot of success.

One thing that kind of boggles me is this: The coaches pick 12 first-team all-Americans in college each year. Yet out of that, only one or two have the ability to play at the international level. It's so hard to get to this level that a player feels very fortunate to be able to take that step up and continue to play.

I've been lucky and fortunate. I can't think of any bad times I have had to overcome compared to a lot of athletes who face surgeries or other health or personal issues. Enduring for this long has been tough at times physically. The body isn't as young as it used to be and doesn't bounce back from training as quickly. But I still have to go in every single day and compete and be intense. This is not like a normal job where a player punches a time clock and then sits at a desk. This requires us to go in and be physical almost all of the time. Plus, there are very good young players constantly coming up, so I have to keep pushing and improving to keep my spot or improve my standing.

This journey has been tough, I can't say that it hasn't been. To be able to get to the point where it all pays off is just an amazing feeling. Very few people realize how hard it is to get to that level to compete for a championship, be it at the Olympic level, college or high school. The journey is what makes it all worth it. Then you reach a high level and are able to show people what you've done to be able to compete for a championship. It takes a lot of hard work. If the heart is not in it, it's going to be a very tiring experience that is wearing both physically and emotionally.

It means a lot to me to have represented my home state, Nebraska, at the state's university. It also means a lot to represent our country. I love the fact that we're able to go overseas and wear "USA" on our shirts. Another great part about the national team is that we get to go see a lot of countries. We consider ourselves ambassadors for our country, and for the areas in which we grew up.

I never forget where I came from, I try to get back home to visit my high school, and get to Lincoln. I owe that to the people who helped me get where I am. I don't feel as though I have any fame, but I do know people, especially back home, are watching me and pulling for me.

This whole experience has been a great ride. We don't get as much publicity as some men's sports, but the support we get is great and we are blessed.

That said, this is a great time for women in athletics. The

women's Olympic basketball team and the U.S. softball team took golds in 1996 and the U.S. women's soccer team has also experienced an incredible year. Those runs laid the groundwork for this incredible roll that women's sports has been on the past few years. I'm hoping women's volleyball will get that kind of recognition. It's important to us to keep paving a path for the girls of today so they can continue to have an opportunity to make their mark when they grow up.

Lessons from sports can be applied to other sports, and to life in general, a job, relationships, other goals. Anyone can get something out of sports if he really believes in what he is doing and is doing it for the right reasons. He doesn't have to be an all-star or even a starter. Do the best with what you have and work hard.

Accomplishing goals in sports can translate into real life because the business world is also all about reaching goals, teamwork, dedication, and trying to be the best.

Something my father said sticks with me: "To be successful, surround yourself with successful people." I've been fortunate in that area because my parents were great. They've been behind me the whole way, and I credit them for a lot of my success. I couldn't have asked for two better parents or coaches than what I've had around me. Everyone I know has had some sort of influence on the person I've become through the years.

STEVEN LOPEZ TAEKWONDO

Name: Steven Lopez
Sport: Taekwondo
Born: Nov. 9, 1978, Manhattan, New York
Family: Parents, Julio and Ondina Lopez; Brothers, Jean and Mark; Sister, Diana
Hometown: Sugar Land, Texas
Resides: Sugar Land, Texas
Trains: Elite Taekwondo Center
Coach: Jean Lopez, Paris Amani

Accomplishments: Six-time national team member; 1996 junior world champion (Barcelona, Spain); 1996 Pan American champion (Havana, Cuba); 1996 USOC. Athlete of the Year; 1997 World Cup champion (Cairo, Egypt); 1998 Pan American champion (Lima, Peru); 1999 Pan American Games champion (Winnipeg, Canada)

Hobbies: Playing other sports, dancing and reading

Post-Olympic goals and plans: Finish college, continue competition, pursue a modeling career, and help continue the tradition of producing champions at the Elite Taekwondo Center

By Steven Lopez

As a younger brother, I did everything that my older brother, Jean, did.

He was really involved in taekwondo, so of course I got into it, too. I had so much fun. I went to tournaments and did pretty well, but again, it was my brother who cleared the path for me to enter the world of taekwondo.

I always wanted to be an Olympic champion. The 2000 Olympic Games in Sydney mark the first time taekwondo is a full medal sport, so it's an exciting time for our sport.

After the 1992 Olympic Games, one of the few athletes in our sport to make a big mark internationally was my brother. So any success I have goes to Jean, my coach Paris Amani, my family, and the Elite Taekwondo Center. Since we train together, our view is that if one of us goes, all of us go. We share that mentality, especially my brother. I really do owe it to him. So if I win an Olympic medal, it is because Jean had a big part of it.

Paris Amani is a former multiple national team member, team captain, and former Olympic Training Center team captain. He is also my coach, who has added invaluable experience, wisdom, and passion. My brother and Paris are responsible for creating the Elite Taekwondo Center and together they make great role models and mentors. They have taken the sport by storm. In only three years Elite has become the premier training center. Athletes from all over the world want to train with us. We all want to give 100 percent, and I think giving 100 percent is the least I can do because of everything my brother and Paris have done.

In 1996 my brother and I made the national team. Unfortunately for us, that year demonstration sports were pulled from the Olympics. It would have been such an honor for us to compete at the Olympic Games in our home country. This situation was out of my hands, so, as painful as it was, I had to let it go. I had to refocus as I was only 17 years old and knew I would have the best opportunity to make history by winning the first official gold medal at the Sydney Olympic Games for our sport. To be part of Olympic history is an awesome feeling. It motivates me to keep going stronger for another four years. The U.S. hasn't produced a world champion since 1973, so that is another goal.

When it was announced that taekwondo would be a medal sport in Sydney, there was a lot of excitement in our sport. To be able to represent the United States means more than mere words could ever describe. Other countries look at the U.S. as being complacent and spoon-fed, but that is not the case. The U.S is a big melting pot of all socioeconomic backgrounds. Other countries unite to cheer against us because they all wish they could be in our shoes and represent the best country in the world. The life they wish for I have in my hands. As an American I feel I have the responsibility and pride to represent this country as an athlete and ambassador.

It's kind of strange that we are now among the stronger countries in taekwondo. It's tough to stay on top. People say they love you, but they really wish you ill will. They come up and say one thing to you, and then say something else behind your back. Canada was the only other English-speaking country when we were in the 1999 Pan American Games. Yet they were rooting against us. But that's something I have to ignore because it is just a waste of energy.

This entire journey has taught me that I can do anything I put my mind to. I'm not the kind who will start something and not finish it. It doesn't matter how long it takes, because if I put my heart into it, I will get it done. That's something that I will one day take into the business world.

An athlete must enjoy the sport, career, or hobby he chooses. If he isn't enjoying it, he will let his training or focus slip and be more likely to quit when he experiences failure. So if a person doesn't like doing something, he probably won't be very good at it. Be passionate about your choice. I wake up in the morning knowing I have three two-hour workouts ahead of me. I love it. Even when I'm just doing a simple kick, I focus and try to improve with each one. That's called looking at the big picture. And since the big picture is made of hundreds or thousands of little pictures, enjoying the journey and keeping focused is very important in order to achieve something special.

While taekwondo has been a huge part of my life, I've never let this or any sport control my life. I focus on what I want to do, but I have to be a well-rounded individual in life. When I look back when I am 40 years old, I will probably remember the small things as much as the big awards. So I don't want to let the rest of my life pass me by and be consumed with my sport. What comes after taekwondo? That's a question I constantly think about. I was in honor society in high school. I know it is important to be balanced physically and mentally. Our mind is like a muscle; if we don't work it, it will fatigue and atrophy.

I've always enjoyed facing the top fighters in our sport. Fighting guys who are not the best will not challenge me to become the best. I like to have students in the university whom I feel can challenge me intellectually and professors who can enlighten me. It is important to have positive people around us. There's nothing worse than having a talented person surrounded by bad coaching, inferior opponents or negative teammates and friends. It kills the will to achieve a person's potential. To reach the top, minimize the negativity and distractions and be in a positive and motivating environment.

This sport has been good to me in terms of traveling. I've been around the world and I'm just 20 years old. I love meeting people from different cultures. I get to see things in person that I have seen in textbooks and on the Discovery Channel. I have seen the pyramids in Egypt, and have visited Australia, Korea, Hong Kong, Argentina, Spain, and Croatia, among other countries. I learned things from those trips that I couldn't learn in a classroom. When I travel I soak everything in like a big sponge. A lot of people who are consumed by the sport let those experiences pass them by. But when their career is done, what do they have to show for it? The medals are nice and important. However, we have a chance to experience things that shape our character through these travels, and I really enjoy it.

Losing is something that is misunderstood and misinterpreted in sports and in life. The label of "loser" should never be applied to someone who suffers a defeat. When we make a mistake, we have a great opportunity to learn. Someone who learns from a defeat or setback is not a loser—he is a winner. There are two choices if you suffer a loss: Quit or find out why you lost. Learn how to lose. That's just the nature of sports and life.

Even champions do not stay on top forever. When an athlete gets to the top, everyone tries to pull him down. So when I win, I look at the video and ask my brother what I could have done to win more decisively or score more points in a particular round. I've had matches that I've won that felt like losses because I didn't do nearly as well as I should have.

So "winning" makes a person no more of a winner than "losing" makes him a loser. It's what we do with the experience that dictates what, and who, we are. We have to be constantly open to improvement. Once we think we know it all we are going to get knocked down, and knocked down hard. I often fight the same guys over and over again, so I don't learn a lot from them. I have to figure out ways to keep them from reading me and find new ways to exploit their weakness and nullify their strengths. That makes me work harder; it's a constant chess game.

I have younger siblings plus all the kids I teach at our taekwondo school. I hope that every time I speak to them I give them sound advice. I want to do whatever I can to help them in the future. Kids are innocent and highly impressionable. I have to give them an honest part of me because I truly want to impact their lives in a positive way.

Sports are important to kids, especially these days. Of course, they need a strong family and good role models, good values and morals. Kids can draw some kind of much-needed structure into their lives from sports. It gives them motivation. Look at the Olympics—countries used to stop wars to compete in them. So sports are very important. Through sports we learn hard work, determination, sacrifice, and the ability to work with others. Those are virtues needed in school, business, and in personal life.

Realizing a dream like winning a gold medal at the Olympics cannot be done alone. For every champion, it takes a number of people behind the scenes who have helped materialize that accomplishment. I am grateful to God and everyone around me for all their support.

KRISTEN MALONEY
GYMNASTICS

Name: Kristen Maloney
Sport: Gymnastics
Born: March 10, 1981, Hacketstown, New Jersey
Family: Parents, Richard and Linda Maloney; Brother, Shawn; Sister, Carrie
Hometown: Pen Argyl, Pennsylvania
Resides: Pen Argyl, Pennsylvania
Trains: Parkettes
Coaches: Bill and Donna Strauss, Robin Netwall, Jack Carter

Accomplishments: 1999 national champion all-around; 1998 national champion all-around; 1998 Goodwill Games gold medalist; 1998 Pacific Alliance Championships (first-team, first all-around, third balance beam, fourth uneven bars); 1997 world championships team, individual event finalist; six years on national teams (1993-1999)

Hobbies: Shopping, listening to music, going to the movies and going out with friends

Post-Olympic goals and plans: Attend UCLA

By Kristen Maloney

Whatever I've accomplished, I credit to the people around me—my family, coaches, teachers, friends, and teammates. They have always been unconditional with their support. They've done an incredible job of staying positive, which, in turn, keeps me that way.

All of that encouragement helps me day after day, year after year. I grew up with my coaches and teammates, and it helps to get that support regularly.

That is among the reasons I've been able to stay in gymnastics. Another reason is that I'm having fun. It is too much of a struggle if it is not enjoyed. It's good for parents and coaches to encourage kids and to guide them through the trying times. But the motivation to excel and stay committed has to come from within. Pushing someone to do something his heart isn't in won't produce a meaningful experience. To be successful requires passion.

I started gymnastics when I was five years old. I had always played with my older brother and sister, but they started school so I didn't have anyone to play with at home. I was always jumping around and doing gymnastics-sorts of things, so my mother put me in a gymnastics class.

I fell in love with the sport very early and always wanted to be in the gym. I got upset if the snow kept me from it. So the passion and love for the sport was born in me from the very beginning.

I didn't have any huge goals in mind at first. I was just taking it one step at a time and improving a little bit each day. Of course there were times when I got frustrated, but with great coaching and encouragement I took another step forward, which increased my desire to work hard and succeed, especially as I grew older.

I progressed through the ranks and was able to go to the Olympic Trials in 1996. I looked around at the company I was in and really had a fun experience, though I did not make the Olympic team. I was able to see how the group that made the team worked hard and competed. They were intense and concentrated on what they had to do. Being with all those girls and competing with them was an honor. I was 15 years old and learned so much from that as to how hard work pays off. It also fueled my desire to compete. It taught me to stay focused and not worry about what's going on around me, not to let the cameras or people take away from the task at hand.

I went to the 1997 world championships. It was motivating, built up my confidence, and gave me the experience I needed for 1998.

In 1998, I won the U.S. nationals. That meant a lot, because I knew all my hard work had paid off. I was dealing with a stress fracture in my shin so I didn't do as well in training as I had hoped leading up to nationals. That made me nervous, because I didn't have as many meets behind me at that point. To be able to compete that well despite the setback from the injury also gave me more confidence.

In 1999, I was fortunate to repeat as the U.S. champion. Knowing that some other gymnasts looked to me for motivation and confidence built my own.

During my career, it's always been very important to me to have a life outside of gymnastics. If I have a bad day at the gym, I don't dwell on it all the time. I move on and focus on other things and then get back at it the next time at the gym. Because I have other interests, when I'm finished competing I won't be saying, "What will I do now?" I have other options that I've worked toward, and I'm looking forward to college at UCLA in 2001.

Education is important because I can't do gymnastics all of my life. There has to be a balance there. I look at education and my social life as important, because those things, along with gymnastics, will help me later in life. An education gives me something not just to fall back on, but to build a future with. Gymnastics can only go so far.

Gymnastics will help later in life, too, even when my career is over. I've learned about dedication and being committed. I've also learned priorities and time management. My schedule is busy, but I make sure I do my homework and take care of my other responsibilities just as I make sure I follow through on my commitment to gymnastics.

Success in school should lead to more success in gymnastics and in whatever else I do, and vice versa.

I have learned not just to set goals, but to enjoy the process. There is a time to be focused and intense. But there is also a time to have fun and enjoy it. I'm living this up because I know it won't last forever.

It's an honor to represent the USA and to know I am one of the best. It makes me feel very proud. I want to do very well and do the best I can. I don't just compete for myself. I compete for my country, my state, my hometown, my gym, parents, coaches, teammates, and friends. It's amazing how many people I am representing.

Being able to travel has really made me appreciate what we have here in the United States. I wouldn't trade this country for anything. I see what others in foreign countries have to deal with. That's also opened my mind to how other people live, their cultures, values, and traditions. It's made me open as a person to other views and cultures.

I also get to interact with a lot of kids. I love kids and since I get to speak to them it's important for me to set a good example. It's important for kids to know that they have role models who work hard and have dedication as they work toward goals.

Sports can be a good learning tool for kids. It's important for them to have fun and learn from the lessons sports teach. As long as they have fun, it doesn't matter how good they are. They don't need to be a world-class athlete to get something out of it. If they set goals and are dedicated, they will be successful. That doesn't have to mean making all-state or winning medals. It means having fun and learning what the experience can teach. Because that is something you can—and should—take with you the rest of your life.

TRIFUN ZIVANOVIC
FIGURE SKATING

Name: Trifun Zivanovic
Sport: Figure Skating
Born: April 17, 1975, Santa Monica, California
Family: Parents, Zoran and Glenda
Resides: Los Angeles, California
Trains: Torrance, California
Coach: Gary Visconti

Accomplishments: 1999 world championships, 16th; 1999 Four Continents Championships, seventh; 1999 U.S. championships, second; 1999 Pacific Coast Sectional, first; 1998 Vienna Cup, second; 1998 Nebelhorn Trophy, first; 1998 U.S. Championships, seventh; 1998 Pacific Coast Sectional, second; 1997 Golden Spin of Zagreb, 2nd; 1997 Pacific Coast Sectional, second; 1996 Piruetten, third; 1996 U.S. championships, seventh; 1996 Pacific Coast Sectional, fourth; 1995 Finlandia Trophy, fourth; 1995 U.S. Olympic Festival, first; 1995 U.S. Junior Championships, second; 1995 Pacific Coast Junior Sectional, first; 1994 U.S.junior championships, sixth; 1994 Pacific Coast Junior Sectional, first; 1994 Southwest Pacific Junior Regional, first; 1993 U.S. junior championships, 11th; 1993 Pacific Coast Junior Sectional, third; 1993 Southwest Pacific Junior Regional, second; 1992 Pacific Coast Novice Sectional, third; 1992 Southwest Pacific Novice Regional, second

Hobbies: Sports memorabilia, music concerts

Post-Olympic goals and plans: Continue to skate, get into coaching

By Trifun Zivanovic

I played ice hockey when I was little and took power skating lessons from a figure skating coach named Gary Visconti.

"You could be a really great skater without the stick and the puck," Visconti said.

I started figure skating and fared pretty well in several local competitions. In 1989, I won the intermediate sectional championship, a much bigger meet than anything I had done. So we figured I could be pretty competitive on a bigger scale.

My father is an auto mechanic. He worked hard carrying heavy engines to support my skating. My mom has backed me emotionally all the way.

When I was 15 and a sophomore in high school in 1991, the dream, and my life, almost ended. We were on Mulholland Drive, a crazy, winding road. My friend, who had just gotten his license, was driving. I tried to put my seatbelt on in the back seat, but it didn't work. The guy sitting next to me, was able to fasten his.

It was about 11 p.m. and the driver was going too fast on a turn. He hit an embankment and the car flipped. The guy sitting next to me grabbed my ankle as I started to fly forward. I thought I was dead. We hit the embankment and after the car came to a rest all I could see was this beige color from all the dust that came from the rocks we hit. I thought all four of us were dead.

I broke my nose pretty badly and hurt my back, but the guy who grabbed my ankle probably saved my life. It hurt my skating career, too. That year, 1991, was supposed to be my first Nationals at the novice level. I had taken sixth in novice sectionals in 1990, so I was looking forward to the 1991 Nationals. But the injuries were serious. I could barely walk and had to maneuver to fit into my desk at school. I didn't skate for almost a year and I seriously thought about quitting. What a loss that would have been had I chosen to hang it up at that point.

I went to Beverly Hills High School; we weren't rich but we lived within the district boundaries. I don't care about the big house and fancy car. I figure if I have that at a young age, what am I going to work toward? How can I enjoy those things at a young age? I didn't have a car, so I rode the bus to school, got a ride or walked. The morning ritual of kids driving up in BMWs, Mercedes, Porsches and fancy sport utility vehicles was amazing.

My high school was good to me because I received physical education credits for skating. It allowed me to train in the morning and come to school late or go to school early and leave to train after lunch.

At my first nationals in 1992 in Orlando, I placed seventh in novice. I was just happy to be there. I wasn't expecting to place high or be in medal contention. The next year I decided to move up to junior, since I was already among the older juniors in just my first year with them.

I made it to nationals, but the result wasn't much better than it had been in novice. I was dead last after the short program. I wanted to go home, but I came back and finished 11th by nailing all my jumps. I didn't have a lot of style or the best package, but the improvement gave me courage to continue. I knew I had hope because of my jumps.

I went through more trying times. When I was a junior in 1994, it was a rough season. I was third at nationals after the short program and dropped to sixth place after the long program. After that competition, I thought, "Why am I doing this? Why am I putting so much into this when all that comes out of it is disappointment?" I came to grips with what happened and realized I skate because I love it. But most years, I had to have that same pep talk with myself at the end of the season.

In 1995, I took second at the junior nationals. My coach at the time told me I had to do well at the upcoming United States Sports Festival if I were to get any international assignments from USFSA. I went to the festival and won, which gave me my first national title. It also led to an international assignment, where I took fourth place.

My first year in seniors was 1996. I took seventh place, which was really good for my first attempt. Internationally, I took third at the 1996 Piruetten, so that was another step forward.

But 1997 was another rough year. I was at the U.S. nationals in Nashville. I just didn't feel right when I got there and was skating badly. We found the reason, a bent blade. We couldn't fix it. We'd straighten it, and it would bend again. Finally, it broke. I didn't have any extra blades. I couldn't follow up at the 1997 nationals after what I had done in my senior debut in 1996. I figured that would destroy my career.

It's no secret that there is a pecking order when trying to get into the higher ranks of seniors. To have to withdraw because of the skate blade problem was devastating. I was close to quitting once again. But I knew I loved the sport, and I knew I could compete with those guys. So I asked myself, "Why am I even contemplating continuing when I should be alongside those guys?"

After Nashville, I realized the real world was staring me in the face.

It was time to blink. I had to face the realities a 21-year-old must face. I needed a job. I decided to continue skating, but I had to work. I got a job delivering pizza. It was really cool and a lot of fun. I skated in the early morning and early afternoon in Torrance, California, and then drove back home and worked in the Westwood and Brentwood areas from 5 p.m. until midnight.

I got home shortly after 1 a.m. and got to bed so I could be at practice early the next morning. Every night I dreamed about getting a medal. And honestly, I knew I could do it.

While I believed I'd be passed over by the United States Figure Skating Association for the international competitions, I received a nice surprise. The USFSA voted to include me in an international assignment.

In 1998, the Olympic year, I took fifth in the short program at the U.S. nationals where there was a lot of talent. I didn't do as well in the long program again, and came out seventh. I wasn't happy. I let a couple of guys get ahead of me that I shouldn't have. I couldn't hold onto fifth, I just let it slip away. A lot of guys got big skating competitions, Grand Prix events, and I was upset because that would've been me had I closed stronger and finished among the top five at nationals. It was back to the drawing board.

I did a Skate Detroit meet after nationals and didn't do too well. But the USFSA officials and international judges were monitoring me for an international competition. They called me upstairs and gave me a lot of great advice. They said I needed to reach out with my artistic ability. So I came home and decided to get an acting coach. The acting coach and I did some work on the stage for the part of Bernardo in "West Side Story." That experience really helped me out.

After the Olympics, a new generation emerges in all the sports as some athletes turn professional and others retire. I got two international assignments from the USFSA. In Germany, I won the title at the Nebelhorn Trophy, which extended the American winning streak at that event to three years. That was a huge boost. So the whole thing turned out better than I had thought.

I went to the Vienna Cup and took second, which gave me another silver medal. I could have won that one, too. Second was very good, but I was upset I had let that one slip away. Still, my international season ended on a high note. Because of the points I accumulated, I was ranked second in the U.S. at that point.

In 1999, I won the Pacific Coast Sectionals senior men's event for the first time. Expectations for me got higher after that, and I wanted a medal at 1999 nationals. The previous year I was seventh; three skaters had left, so I was pegged to take fourth. Any of the four medals, gold through bronze, plus the pewter they give to fourth place, would have done me just fine, especially considering everything I'd been through.

After the short program I was in third place. I was worried because I had been high in the short program so many times before only to let it slip and fall.

"I have to hold on to it," I thought. "I can't go down from here."

I approached my long program differently. I thought, "This is the first half of my dream, I have to finish. I was delivering pizza last year, for goodness sakes. Come on, finish it off. Go for it!"

I didn't just finish it off and hold my placing, I improved my standing one spot into second for the final placings. I won the silver medal. My whole family was there, along with my girlfriend. That meant a lot. It was at the Delta Center in Salt Lake City, which is a huge place. But I could see my girlfriend and my mom.

That silver medal was very special. Nobody ever thought I could get second at nationals. If you asked anyone, even people around where I train, they would never have forecasted such a high finish.

Understand where I'm from. My father emigrated from Yugoslavia in the 1970s. He has worked hard and provided everything we've needed, but the odds were still against me.

My mother has been a wonderful inspiration for me. Having muscular dystrophy is rough for her, but she never complains. She's always made sure the skating bill was paid. While the times have been tough, there was never a day where I showed up at the rink and heard, "The bill's not paid, you can't skate."

My mother takes care of me before she takes care of herself. It's really hard; she's not able to jump up and go with me like she used to because she's confined to a wheelchair. With that disease, it gradually gets worse. When I was young, I remember her running around and jumping in the car to go somewhere with me. But she doesn't give up. She's hung on for so many years. I still don't see her giving up. While she is different physically, I recognize the spirit she still has, and that is amazing.

It feels good to have put together a good career. People have said "forget it" so many times over the years. I kept bouncing back, and that showed me that I have more perseverance and resilience than I thought was possible.

I love skating. I love to compete and put my neck on the line. One of my favorite things is traveling to all the different countries of the world. And I've had a great time with skating. I wouldn't have done it any other way aside from the directions my career has taken me. If someone said, "You can do it over—take this quicker route by doing this and that," I would say, "Forget it. I don't want any part of that."

A lot of the guys who used to beat me either aren't competing any longer or I have passed them. They used to be better than I was and got to go to all the international events. Now I'm the one who gets to do those things, especially after the silver medal at the 1999 U.S. championships.

The message I have is to love what you're doing. Even the adversity provides growth. I would definitely say that the adversity has helped me, not hurt me. When everything is going perfectly it's easy to be happy. But most of the time it doesn't work that way. If we are proud of ourselves, and are doing the best we can, that is real—something we can be proud of. To be a true champion, we have to be happy to be out there even when the chips are down.

JOSH DAVIS
SWIMMING

Name: Josh Davis
Sport: Swimming
Born: Sept. 1, 1972, San Antonio, Texas
Family: Wife, Shantel; Son, Caleb; Daughter, Abby
Resides: Austin, Texas
Hometown: San Antonio, Texas
Trains: University of Texas
Coach: Eddie Reese

Accomplishments: Triple gold medalist at 1996 Olympic Games, the most gold medals by any man in the entire Games; 1998 world championship team captain; earned four golds and a bronze at 1995 World University Games and three gold medals and a bronze at 1995 Pan Am Games; holds three short-course American records (200m free, 100m and 200m individual medley); 1993 Pan Pacific and NCAA champion in 200m free; seven-time national champion

Hobbies: Time with family, speaking to kids, reading the Bible

Post-Olympic goals and plans: Stay involved with swimming

By Josh Davis

My first experience with the Olympics was watching the 1984 Los Angeles Games on television when I was 12. I remember sitting in my living room watching the men's 4x200-meter freestyle relay and seeing the U.S. men overcome insurmountable odds to win the gold. I thought, wouldn't that be neat to be an Olympian. Even though I liked swimming, I was too busy with other sports so I didn't consider training and racing until the following year.

I was 13 when my best friend Murray encouraged me to join an all-year swim club. Being a novice, my strokes were not very good. My freestyle and backstroke were OK, but my butterfly was terrible and breaststroke wasn't even legal. Unfortunately, I inferred from this coach that I should switch sports.

After talking with my parents, we decided instead of switching sports to switch coaches. It's amazing what happens with a new coach. A great coach is someone who believes in you, encourages you, and teaches you truth on how you can be your very best.

My new coach, Jim Yates, taught me all the big and little things that it takes to become an elite athlete: technique, streamlining, intensity, strategy, nutrition, flexibility, etc. Sure enough, these things began to work. Soon after, I went from novice to Texas state champion in the 200m free by the time I was 15.

That was the same year that I was inspired by Matt Biondi in the 1988 Seoul Olympics. I taped all of his swims and I watched them almost every day. I learned so much from watching the great ones and then at practice I tried to imitate them. That was the year Biondi set the American record in the 200m free with a time of 1:47.7 seconds. With the direction of my coach and the inspiration of Olympians like Matt, I set a goal to become the best 200m freestyler I could be.

In 1990, I moved from one great coach to another. I began training at the University of Texas under Olympic coach Eddie Reese. My freshman year our team won the '91 NCAA swimming championship in our own pool in Austin. It was awesome!

Many athletes pride themselves on training hard, but unfortunately, when the season is over, especially if they win, some pride themselves on partying hard as well. Afraid of being rejected and lacking in character, I chose to party also. After drinking too much, studying late hours, and training, my body broke down and I became very sick. When school got out May 15, I went home and stayed in bed for two weeks.

We all know how frustrating it is to be sick, but to be stuck in bed for that long made me analyze my life. I thought to myself, "I have everything society says I'm supposed to have to be happy: my national championship ring, making good grades, my name is in the newspaper, and I'm a popular guy on the team. But here I am stuck in bed, can't even move, and I'm completely empty and unsatisfied on the inside."

It was a "bottom of the barrel" experience. God had allowed me to get to a point in my life where He had my attention. As best I knew how I said a simple prayer. Prayer is not really the words I say but the genuine attitude of my heart. Laying in bed, the attitude of my heart and genuine desire was to have God change me. I asked Him to change this situation, change my life and to make me the kind of man He created me to be.

It was that season of my life where God gave me the strength and courage to respond to His truth—Jesus Christ is exactly who He says He is and that He is worthy of my full trust in every area of my life. I can trust Him with swimming, school, and my social life, every hour of the week, not just Sunday mornings. In a way, Jesus Christ was my new "Head Coach." It's amazing what happens when you get a great coach! Remember, a great coach is someone who believes in you, encourages you, and gives you truth so that you can be your very best.

Jesus Christ is the best coach ever. I realized that I could talk to Him anytime and read His message to me in the Bible. For the first time, it was a real and personal relationship. It wasn't a crutch, religion, or an emotional experience; it was a new and real friendship. I told God that I never wanted to go back living in my own power according to the world's ways.

My freshman year I had two new coaches, Eddie Reese and Jesus Christ. I listened to Eddie to train my body and I listened to Jesus to train my spirit. What God communicated to me through the Bible was that my character is more important than my worldly success. I learned He loves me so much that He doesn't want anything getting in the way of our relationship. I would need to be reminded this truth many times throughout my career but I knew that I now had God's direction and peace.

Looking back on 1992, I knew God was preparing my character for something in the future. That was the year I raced at my first Olympic Trials, the most pressure-filled meet in the world. Many consider the U.S. Trials to be more intense than the Olympics themselves. Every four years there's one night, in a race just over a minute long, that you have to finish first or second. If it's an off day, too bad, better luck four years later. I felt very young, was very nervous, and didn't swim as I had hoped. However, I set a goal that I would be at the 1996 U.S. Trials prepared for the pressure and ready to make the Olympic team.

In 1994, my senior year, I moved up in the world rankings from fourth to first. Things were looking good as we headed into the year of the Centennial Olympic Games. But first were the Olympic Trials.

In March 1996, all the fastest swimmers in the U.S. gathered to see who was the best to represent us in the Olympic Games. Exactly a year before the Trials, the Texas assistant swim coach, Kris Kubik, gave me a small picture of an Olympic gold medal to put in my wallet. To me, it was a reminder of why I was training so hard and also a reminder to ask God to continue to mold my character and to give me peace in the midst of the pressure. All my prayers were answered at the Trials. Even in the middle of all the pressure and expectations, I had this confident peace that I would make the team and things would work out fine. I qualified in three events, the 200m free, the 4x200m free relay and 4x100m free relay.

Just to have competed in the Olympics is a tremendous honor in itself! I realized that honor when I finished seventh in my individual race in the 200m free. At first, I was disappointed because I was concerned about what the media and others would say. But I knew I had done my very best at that moment, and I was extremely proud to have represented my family and country. Besides, seventh in the world is pretty good. Although content, I could never have imagined what God had in store for me on the relays.

My next event was the 4x200m free relay. We were the underdogs and described by the media as lucky to get third. We ended up winning by a landslide! Receiving that gold medal and singing our national anthem was almost as good as marrying Shantel. After that was the sprint relay, the 4x100m free relay. The pressure was amazing. America had never lost this relay in Olympic history, and now the Russians had their fastest relay ever assembled ready to break our streak. We came from behind and beat them and busted the Olympic record in the process! I had now received a second gold medal.

What was significant about that sprint relay performance was our respective splits. Jon Olsen, our captain, led off in 49.9 seconds, I was the second leg with a 49.00; Brad Schumacher was 49.01; and our anchor Gary Hall Jr. had the fastest split ever at the time with a 47.4. Whoever had the fastest split would anchor the third and final relay, the medley relay. The second fastest swimmer would anchor the morning prelim relay.

If the final relay wins, then the prelim relay also gets awarded a gold medal. Because my split was .01 second faster than Brad's, the coaches decided to put me on the prelim relay. At night the final relay easily won the gold medal, breaking the world record by an astonishing two seconds. I was awarded my third gold medal. I had the great blessing of being the only male in any sport at the 1996 Olympic Games to get three gold medals.

Do you think I was glad that I listened to my coaches about technique and streamlining? Do you think I was glad that I tried to make every start, turn, and stroke perfect in practice? Do you think I was glad I had God's peace?

God had been preparing my character all those years for just such a time. He used my coaches, Eddie Reese and Kris Kubik, to help prepare me physically. He used Shantel to encourage me emotionally. And He used His Word and many Christians to strengthen me spiritually.

My story is unique in that God taught me lessons through situations like the Olympics where the world is watching. But the fact is, God teaches all of us lessons. He wants all of us to know Him more, entrust our lives to Him, and make Him our "Head Coach." Who is your Head Coach?

BARB KUNKEL
TAEKWONDO

Name: Barb Kunkel
Sport: Taekwondo
Born: Sept. 17, 1969, Tacoma, Washington
Family: Parents, Roy Kunkel and Peggy Guizzetti Kunkel; Siblings, Julie Kunkel, Roger Kunkel, Rachelle Kunkel-Baker, Jeremy Kunkel
Hometown: Tacoma, Washington
Resides: Colorado Springs, Colorado
Trains: Olympic Training Center
Coach: Han Won Lee

Accomplishments: 1999 Pan Am Games Team Trials, gold medal; 1999 U.S. Olympic/Pan Am Weight Divisions Championships, bronze medal; 1998 Pan American Taekwondo Championship, gold medal; 1998 U.S. National Team Trials, gold medal; 1998 U.S. nationals, silver medal

Hobbies: Sports, church, teaching

Post-Olympic goals and plans: To own my own business, teach and coach taekwondo and help others achieve their dreams in sports and life.

By Barb Kunkel

My dreams in sports had always been centered on basketball. I had an offer for a scholarship to play college basketball in New York, but because of finances, I accepted a scholarship to Highline Junior College, near my hometown of Tacoma.

In 1987 during my freshman year, we were at a tournament in Oregon. I took an outlet pass and was crushed by two people. I fell down hard, but I didn't know anything was wrong. My knee started giving out, but I just walked it off each time and it seemed to be better, until it gave out again and again. I didn't want to accept the fact that I was injured. I played like this for about a month.

Finally, my coach looked at me.

"I can't play you anymore," he said.

"I understand," I said. Reality was beginning to set in.

He knew that it wasn't normal for my knee to continually give out, but we were still optimistic. We thought I just needed arthroscopic surgery. The rehab period, I was told, was two weeks. To an athlete injured for the first time, two weeks seems like a lifetime, but it was something I had to do.

When the surgery began, the doctor stopped relatively shortly into it.

"We can't do just this," he said. "The damage is extensive, and I have to open you up, full reconstructive surgery is needed."

I was thunderstruck. I didn't know what to say, except, "How long?"

"About a month or so," the doctor replied.

I groaned, but knew I had no choice. I was already there under the knife so I might as well do it. "OK," I said, "Just do it."

In post-op, I was given the news that the rehabilitation would take a year. Things seemed to be only getting worse. I was upset, yet determined to shorten the time.

I pushed hard in rehab. I went to sports therapy three days a week and I was in the water every day, wanting to do more. The first rehab for an athlete is probably the toughest, because up to that point everything had been positive. We have a tendency to take things such as life, family, and health for granted until we lose it. That's just how we are in America, because our life is so fast paced. Since we have the instant gratification mentality, taking a step back can be really traumatic.

The rehabilitation taught me a lot. A person can do anything if he really believes and really wants to do it. At a recent taekwondo camp I met a participant with a prosthetic leg. She was amazing. I told this young woman what an inspiration she was to me. She showed me that a person can always find a way to pursue something he is passionate about. Weaknesses or special challenges can be overcome with the right attitude and pursuing heart.

A big issue these days is the mentality of many people.

We must take "can't" out of the vocabulary. To me, the definition of "can't" is this: Zero-percent effort. If I say, "I can't" in regard to something, then I'm probably right, I won't do it. Don't let the adversity overcome you without even trying.

"Can't" is a cop-out, a quick one-word way to quit. Instead, it is better to say, "It is difficult, but I am going to try." This statement will put you much further ahead in the game of life than a cop-out answer.

The following basketball season, I was rebounding against a taller girl. She came down on top of me, my other knee gave out and I tore the ligaments in my left knee. I knew exactly what had happened, and wild, frustrating thoughts started racing through my head. "Why me? I just came back, I don't understand."

I believe I paid too much attention to my injured leg and not enough to my healthy one after the surgery, and that directly led to blowing out the other knee.

"I don't know if you are going to play competitive basketball any more," the doctor told me.

"You can't do this," I replied. "This is my life!" I was angry and did not understand what was happening to me. Athletics was everything. Why was it being taken from me? What did I do to deserve this?

After the second surgery the doctor decided to put a cast on me because it was remembered how hard I pushed the rehab the first time.

The doctor said, "If this happens again you may not be able to walk again, so be smart."

"I will play again. You'll see," I thought to myself.

I decided to get a job and work out at the local health club in the evenings. I did not want this to get the best of me.

Between doing rehab, swimming, and racquetball every day I

was able to play basketball with some college guys. I was determined to come back and play competitive basketball again. After I got my fill of fitness each day, I took two young kids to their karate class each night, and I just sat and observed. The more I watched the more I liked it, and I decided that I could use it to help me get back in shape for basketball. Also, it was free, and I had to get fit again.

Each day I woke up bright and early and headed off to work managing an airline catering company from 6 a.m. to 2:30 p.m. Then I worked out and played basketball or racquetball the rest of the afternoon until karate class from 9 p.m. to 10 p.m. I liked it so much that I couldn't get enough of it. I stayed an hour later every day to get extra instruction. There was something different about this sport. It was great.

After doing that for about six months, I noticed that there was a taekwondo school across the street.

"I have to check this out," I thought to myself.

I went in and sat down. I couldn't believe how hard those people were working. All of the students were Korean, as was the instructor, Sang Hyuk Cha. I showed up every day and watched. After a month, the instructor's wife talked to me.

"Are you going to join or are you just going to keep showing up and watching?" she asked.

I joined and was Master Cha's first American student and as well as one of his first female students. I was told he didn't like to teach females, especially American ones, but I always liked a challenge, so I was determined to make him teach me. I worked harder than everyone, getting to the studio at 3 p.m. and staying until 10 p.m.

At first we couldn't communicate very well because he spoke Korean and I spoke English, so one of my Korean friends helped interpret and worked with me each day. To increase my learning opportunity I started Korean school, not a language school, but an actual elementary school for Korean kids. I knew that was the best way to learn the language. I had taught myself how to read and write Korean through books and tapes, but I knew I had to learn in a more practical environment. Plus, I wanted to learn more about the culture.

It was so much fun.

Many times we learn languages in school and more than likely never use them again. This was something that I knew I'd use for a lifetime. I've been to Korea eight times and being able to communicate has made those trips so much more meaningful and enjoyable.

In Korean school, I was put in kindergarten. You know those tiny chairs kindergartners sit in? I had to sit in one of those. It was hysterical, a 20-year-old with the four- to five-year-olds. All the kids laughed and looked at me. The teachers found out I learned a lot on my own already, so I was given a test and then moved up to the sixth grade. Which was funny too, because many of these young kids were learning taekwondo at Master Cha's studio. They didn't mind though, they loved helping me with my Korean school homework.

That helped me learn how to communicate better with Master Cha, and I started to teach him English.

Master Cha is a 17-time Korean national champion. He is well known from his taekwondo career, he is focused and disciplined, and is never satisfied with second best. He emphasizes that to me.

Between the support of my family and the guidance of Master Cha, I reached an elite level rather quickly. My mother and Master Cha helped instill the competitive spirit and focus needed to become the best. Since I grew up being involved in so many different sports, I learned the importance of goal setting and what is needed to achieve my best, simply by the nature of competition and getting better.

I wanted to be the same way at taekwondo, so much so that I'd stay late every single night to practice. One night, Master Cha walked up to me.

"Here's your own key," he said. "You're always the last one here anyway. Lock up when you leave."

There are a lot of aspects about taekwondo that appeal to me. I like the kicking and fighting. The kicking is something that I really think is appealing. So many people are used to just using their hands. If someone punches you in the face, what's the first reaction? To punch them back. Not many people use their legs, yet they are more powerful than hands and you can catch someone off-guard. Taekwondo teaches how to kick to the face and in the air without dropping, and that is just amazing to me. The ability to kick and to know how to kick correctly is just awesome.

Another good factor about taekwondo is that it gives people self-confidence and teaches discipline and respect. And if a person already has self-confidence, discipline, and respect, it gives him more, which allows more to be achieved in life. You compete against yourself.

My doctor thought I was crazy for doing taekwondo. But my knees didn't hurt and were actually getting strengthened and becoming more flexible. Another reality was that my basketball career was coming to an end, at least from a competitive, organized standpoint. I had a job that I liked and didn't really have time to be a full-time college basketball player. There was no WNBA (women's professional basketball) back then, so my career would have ended after a couple more years anyway. With taekwondo, I knew I had found something that I could do for years.

My first year on the U.S. national taekwondo team was 1993. I had no clue that I had even made the team. There's a funny story behind that.

I went to nationals that year, and I took third place at the competition. I was really excited because that qualified me to go to the U.S. Team Trials in Chicago. My instructor told me, "Don't expect anything. Just get some experience, and do your best."

With that in mind I trained even harder, and I went to the trials and won. I was happy, but everyone around me was ecstatic, jumping around and high-fiving each other when they won. I didn't realize the significance of my win until I was on my way home from the airport when I realized I would have to ask for six weeks off from work. I was scared but ecstatic as I realized I had just made the U.S. national team. I was so new to the sport and the U.S. Taekwondo

Association that I didn't even know I had made the national team! I was just in it for the love of the sport and the love for competition.

After making the team I had the opportunity to travel abroad and compete for the U.S.—an opportunity to see the world and learn about other cultures first hand. All the while I was doing something I loved. As I traveled abroad, I gained a new respect for the U.S. and the privileges and great opportunities we have here.

As time went on, the 1996 Olympics were approaching. We were excited, because the taekwondo had been a demonstration sport in 1988 and 1992 and now we were training to compete in the 1996 Games in Atlanta, our home ground.

Coach Han Lee, the U.S. national team coach, as well as a two-time U.S. Olympian and Olympic bronze medalist, asked me to move to the Olympic Training Center in Colorado Springs in 1995. He trained us harder than I ever had before. Each day we trained from 6 to 7:30 a.m. for conditioning, then we ate and slept for a short period of time. We assembled from 9:30 to 11:30 and again from 2 to 4 p.m. to train in taekwondo.

The following year he guided me to make the team for a fourth time, and also brought me to a new level where I achieved a World University Games gold medal, a U.S. Open gold medal, and a Denmark Open gold medal.

But something happened. For some reason, and I've never heard the explanation for it, taekwondo was not part of the 1996 Olympic Games. It crushed us, especially the older athletes. We had trained so hard for this moment, and the competitive window, because of age or other commitments, was closing.

I knew I wanted to continue in the sport, but I wasn't sure if I wanted to continue on the Olympic path. I prayed about it so much, and so did many people close to me.

My coach, with his remarkable experience and background stated, "It is a great feeling to get a gold medal for your country, but the greatest feeling of all is representing your country in the Olympic Games. The whole world is watching and there is no greater feeling than that."

One of my quotations is, "Dream big and never let go of your dreams." By living at the Olympic Training Center, I am surrounded with winners, people who have the same goals as I do. Being surrounded by negative, non-supporting people eventually gets to a person. After a while, she will start believing it, especially when she is vulnerable, like after a bad competition, an injury or personal issues. Therefore, I tell people to surround themselves with people they want to be like. You will become like the environment you hang out in.

As a Christian, this whole experience has been exciting for me, from the knee injuries to sort of stumbling, so to speak, into taekwondo. I look at things and think, "Why am I here?" There have been so many opportunities to go down a different path, yet I kept pushing on and weathered the storms.

In the 1996 team trials, I hurt my leg, not related to my knee injuries, late in the competition. I couldn't use my left leg at all. I was undefeated that year going into the finals. I only had to win one more. I asked the trainer to tape me up tight and then proceeded to the ring. I was worried.

My coach, Han Won Lee, told me, "Fight smart and with heart. You don't need all of your tools to win. If you fight smart and with heart, you can overcome anything. Attack their weakness, and avoid their strengths."

I realize those are words to live by in not only sports, but in life. In the match to make the team, I only kicked four or five times in nine minutes because of my injury. Still, I won because of the mental game and because I chose my shots and executed everything else well. I was focused beyond belief. It's so amazing how we can win with a strong mental attitude even when we are facing someone of equal or better physical ability or an unexpected challenge.

Taekwondo is a lifetime sport, whereas in most sports, an athlete is only able to compete for a certain number of years, especially at a high level of competition.

DAN O'BRIEN
DECATHLON

Name: Dan O'Brien
Sport: Decathlon
Born: July 18, 1966, Portland, Oregon
Family: Parents, Virginia and Jim O'Brien; Sisters, Kathy Fox, Karen Serna, Laura Buckle, Patricia O'Brien, Sara O'Brien; Brothers, Scott Farrar, Tom O'Brien
Resides: Moscow, Idaho
Coach: Rick Sloan

Accomplishments: Gold medal, 1998 Goodwill Games; gold medal, 1996 Olympics, Atlanta; set world record at Talence, France, decathlon, 1992; world champion in the decathlon, 1991, 1993 and 1995; ranked No. 1 in the world in the decathlon by *Track & Field News,* 1991-1996; gold medalist, 1994 Goodwill Games; U.S. champion in decathlon, 1991, 1993, 1994, 1995, 1996; Champion, IAAF World Athletic Championships in heptathlon, 1993; set world record in heptathlon, 1993

Hobbies: Reading

Post-Olympic goals and plans: Pondering several options

By Dan O'Brien

Part of what keeps me going is that my event, the decathlon, is very difficult. There are so many things to master.

Everyone asks, "Are you going to retire soon?" I'm not quitting until I think I've gotten everything out of this sport that I can.

The decathlon is, to me, like a round of golf. I've had several good holes here and there, but I haven't had the perfect round I could have by stringing together an entire round of good holes. That is the challenge in the decathlon. I want to "play the perfect round," but it is not an easy thing. I've had competitions where I've done very well in seven or eight events, but never all ten at the same time.

So there is still something left for me to accomplish. I don't want to look back when I'm 50 years old and say, "You know, if I'd have just trained a little harder..."

I want to do it all before I am done. So I'm still competing, even though in July 1999 I had surgery on my knee for a patella tendon. Another setback . . . big deal, life in any arena is full of adversity. The sun will rise tomorrow, and so will I. The clouds have to part at some point and sometimes we have to push them out of the way to see the sun shine. My goal is to go back and win again.

One of the keys to success is being a good loser in order to win. We have to learn to deal with things that don't go exactly the way we want. We have to understand that this is a process in sports, like in life. For me, it has taken years, perhaps even a decade, to figure it out.

My coach, Rick Sloan, and I truly believe the reason we are successful is that we forget about everything else and concentrate on the preparation. The day-to-day training and preparation is the most important thing. It's even more important than the major competitions because it is the day-to-day, month-to-month, year-to-year training that we make the biggest sacrifices for. I've had consecutive years of not being able to spend more time with friends, not having a girlfriend, or not seeing family on holidays. We need to have other interests but by the same token we have to make sacrifices that are necessary if we are to reach our potential.

I gained a lot of notoriety before the 1992 Olympics. I was favored to medal yet I didn't even qualify because of a couple of fluke instances. I went into the Olympic Trials without a Plan B; that is, I wasn't prepared for everything that I should have been. I had to come back with a Plan B to eliminate those mistakes and not let them drag me down the next time.

It wasn't such a terrible thing not making the 1992 Games. I was just beginning my career, and since I was a young athlete, I still had a lot ahead of me. I overcame it by setting a positive tone for the next four years. I turned it into a positive because I let it motivate me.

I ended up doing some television commentating for the Olympics in 1992. At the time, I realized the Olympics are high pressure and high stress. While I wanted to be out there, I was glad I wasn't going through it. I would have loved to win gold that year. But I think it was my mission to sit and watch it that one time.

My career had gone along very smoothly to that point; I had a couple of national championships and a world championship the year before in 1991. I was due for a setback. That helped me develop that hunger that says, "This isn't just something I want to do. I have to do it!"

I learned more from that failure than I could have ever learned from any success. I didn't realize until later how many people were pulling for me or who had similar stories of overcoming some sort of adversity. All the cards, letters, and phone calls I received really made an impression on me.

There is a need in the U.S for people to develop and create heroes. My event is especially interesting to the public during Olympic years because the decathlon itself is a form of adversity, with all the different events and the way things can happen to change standings, and futures, in a heartbeat.

Not until after the 1992 Olympics did I realize that people were pulling for me and that kids were looking up to me. There is a need for athletes to be role models in this day and age. I have no problem taking on that role. I enjoy answering questions from kids and talking to parents. We can all learn a lot from one another. That's an important point for me, too. I can learn from the people who tell me their stories. While they might not get the media coverage or public attention, their stories often inspire me and lend perspective, especially when I face a challenge.

I draw strength from people who tell me they have followed me and cheered me on. The feeling I get when a kid comes up and asks for my autograph is so special. I was always quiet and introverted on the field, letting the pressure get to me. I learned over the years that a lot of people pull for me. That and the love I have for the sport push me on. I remember when I was younger running on dirt tracks and vaulting with stiff, old poles. But I always had fun, just like I do now. If I have fun when I compete, I block out all the pressure and other factors that can work against me in competition.

I think the role-model status extends to all professions. Successful doctors, teachers, lawyers, or whatever, have the responsibility to set a good example. If our success can help someone else achieve success, then our success is that much more meaningful. And the effect we have is long lasting.

That helped me keep pushing forward. For me, that was just part of the game, to continue moving on. I had a lot of reasons to quit. But for a lot of us athletes, we can think of no other place to go at that point. I had to get to Atlanta in 1996 for the Olympics. What happened in 1992 was the driving force behind what I would accomplish in the coming years.

Another one of the reasons I have stayed in the sport is we now have an opportunity to make a living as athletes. So I believe I am destined to draw my career out as far as it goes. With that comes the responsibility of being prepared and representing our country and the people around me with excellence.

I love the everyday training. I don't do it to inspire other people, or because it inspires me. I keep working, sweating, and pushing the envelope because I enjoy doing it. That being said, I am grateful and very happy that I can inspire others. It's nice to know what I do with my passion can motivate and inspire other people.

Success comes with a price—it is called discipline and determination, and it's needed when we face adversity. Bruce Lee had that kind of theory, that to master anything there are obstacles to overcome and disciplines to incorporate.

Look at anyone who has achieved a level of meaningful success, and you will see that he had adversity to overcome at some point. We see a couple of kids come out of high school and make it right to the NBA with multimillion-dollar contracts. But it's not all positive. They either had an adversity in the past or will face adversity caused by their meteoric rise that they will have to overcome. It's just never as easy as it seems. No one is born a "great" athlete. Some of the best athletes in the world started with almost nothing, yet pushed ahead and became successful.

When an athlete achieves that success, it is a small moment in time compared to what it took to get there. That's a big part of my success, enjoying the journey, and realizing the importance of it. I like lifting weights and working out. Every single day I have fun. The hardest part is the journey. The destination is only a result of that journey. The competitions are stressful, and that's when I have had thoughts of quitting.

But if we truly love the journey, we will discover things inside that show us the journey is where the character is built. Standing on the podium with a medal around my neck is an incredible rush, but it is the times alone, or with my coach on the track, or in the gym, that are important. Those are the moments no one sees. But without hundreds and thousands of those moments, you won't stand on the podium even a single time.

The decathlon is something that tests me every day. Just when I start to feel good about myself, I fall down in the hurdles or break a pole in the pole vault and realize I am not an expert. This event is humbling daily. I don't have to be great in one thing, but on the other hand I have to be good in every single thing.

What that tells me about myself is that I only get what I give. The more I can give, the more I will get. How much pain can I take—the healthy kind of pain—to dig deep and push beyond what I've done? How much can I sacrifice to get where I want to go? That's the way it is in life, too.

The last few years I have realized I must have a life outside of track and field. I've found a better balance with my life and that has even helped me enjoy the sport itself more.

Not everyone is destined for Olympic gold, or even first place at a high school meet. The decathlon has taught me that finishing is a victory, regardless of where I place. I watch a decathlon and I see the last event, the 1,500-meter run, and the guys who came in fourth or lower are smiling and giving high fives. That's because they have once again defeated the decathlon. We don't have to take first prize to be a winner. We have to achieve what we believe we can realistically attain. If we do that, we have a golden feeling, and reaching that potential is an Olympian accomplishment.

One thing that bothers me is watching a state championship high school event. I see the kids crying after they lose. Why are they crying? They were second best in the whole state. A lot of kids had to meet or exceed their potential to reach that level, so there should be a feeling of celebration, not personal annihilation. There's no reason to feel sad when we come up one game short. We won because of the participation itself, the commitment and the sacrifice.

I tell kids not to let sports consume them. I think they should try everything in school. I played in the school band, was in the chess club, and even did some drama club activities. I played the trumpet for ten years and I loved being in band. I wouldn't have found track and field had I not been looking to try everything. I really respect my parents for that. I find it difficult to see kids who play one sport year round and never try anything else. I was pretty small and skinny as a kid. It wasn't until my sophomore year of high school that my parents let me play football for fear I'd get crushed. I also played basketball, and I still love that sport. In college, I played pick-up basketball year round. I used to love getting down to the gym for "noon ball" with the guys.

Another key to success in anything is surrounding yourself with people who are positive and share your vision. I can honestly say I wouldn't have gone this far without having people who care about me as a person. Also, I attribute all the success I've had to the coaches throughout my career. I can only do what I am taught. I am good at taking direction. Even natural athletes have to learn from somebody.

In 1996, I was determined not just to qualify for the Olympics, but to win the gold medal. I won the gold medal in Atlanta. People said, "It must've been awesome to get that gold medal." Sure it was. But I went there with a mission. I wasn't at all surprised that I got the gold because I had done everything in my power to prepare for those Olympic Games. To tell you the truth, I was more relieved than thrilled because everything turned out the way I wanted. It was more victorious than glorious. Good athletes expect that success. They train for it and expect it, so it's not quite as surprising to them when they win as it is to other people.

Winning the gold medal in 1996 was also a huge weight off of my shoulders after what had happened in 1992. It also realized a long-time goal of mine to be an Olympic athlete.

One of my dreams as a kid was to be an Olympian. I saw the Americans beat the Russians in ice hockey during the 1980 Olympics in Lake Placid. I vowed from that day on that I'd represent the U.S. I didn't think there was anything more thrilling. In track and field, it is more personal than team-oriented. Because of the way it is set up, when we step on the field some of our biggest nemeses and adversaries are Americans. Track and field in the U.S. sets up a lot of competition between Americans. I don't really feel like a team as a result of that. But when it comes to representing our country, I believe we all do that proudly.

I've been around the world several times over for competition. While other countries have more support and financial resources for their athletes in some cases, I'm glad I'm training in the U.S. because I can set things up the way I want to. I don't have to be told what I can or have to do every step of the way. So there is good and bad in it. I take the good because as Americans we have the ultimate good thing—freedom.

Businesses have talked in recent years about employees having ownership and autonomy in the company. That's the way life in the U.S. is. But that ownership means we will only achieve what we set out to achieve. We have to be willing to do the work. There is a certain discipline in that. That's why the lack of discipline in this country in certain areas hurts us. No one else will achieve it for us; it has to come from within.

That's why I surround myself with people like my coach and why I've been fortunate to have great family members and friends supporting me. My coach requires every bit of effort I have every day, and I have to push to reach that.

The decathlon is set up like life: You have a good or bad event, and what do you do? You move on to the next one. The greatest attribute an athlete can have is to forget about what just happened. It doesn't matter whether he just won or lost, because that result won't have an impact on what's coming up.

You have to have the ability to focus for a long time. How can Michael Jordan be so good, and go up for a shot and forget about everything else? How can he shoot with the game on the line when flashes are going off, or if he's missed three shots in a row leading up to that one? Why did he always seem to make that last, most important shot? Because he would forget about everything else and focus on what he had to do.

The gun goes off, and we race for the finish line. The saying about that is that there is "one moment in time." That moment is a short period. We have to look forward, or it will pass us by. Seize the moment and savor it. Then pick up and move on to the next challenge. It is waiting.